WHERE COURAGE IS LIKE A WILD HORSE

WHERE COURAGE IS LIKE A WILD HORSE

The World of an Indian Orphanage

Sharon Skolnick (Okee-Chee)
and Manny Skolnick

University of Nebraska Press
Lincoln and London

©1997 by the University of Nebraska Press
All rights reserved. Manufactured in the
United States of America. ∞ The paper in this
book meets the minimum requirements of
American National Standard for Information
Sciences – Permanence of Paper for Printed
Library Materials, ANSI z39.48-1984.
Library of Congress Cataloging-in-
Publication Data: Skolnick, Sharon, 1944–
Where courage is like a wild horse :
the world of an Indian orphanage / Sharon
Skolnick (Okee-Chee) and Manny Skolnick.
p.   cm. ISBN 0-8032-4263-8 (cl : alk. paper)
1. Skolnick, Sharon, 1944– .
2. Chiricahua Indians – Biography.
3. Murrow Indian Orphanage.
4. Indian children – Oklahoma –
Social conditions.
I. Skolnick, Manny, 1946– .
II. Title. E99.c68s53   1998
976.6 ́004972 – dc21
97-2094
CIP

To Lynette Perry, the mother who lifted
two scared little Apache girls out of
the orphanage by the strength of her love.
I love you, Mom.

CONTENTS

Contents

The girl you'll meet in these pages has become, in 1996, a fifty-two-year-old woman named Sharon Skolnick. My Indian name, by which I am perhaps better known, is Okee-Chee. I've lived half my life in Chicago, where I have raised my family of four children and, now, four grandchildren. My family owns and operates the only American Indian–owned art gallery in Chicago; I am a painter, doll maker, and craftswoman of some reputation. I've been lucky enough to see some of my dreams come true.

Four decades ago this summary of my life seemed unlikely. In 1953 I was a ward of the state of Oklahoma, living with my sister in the Murrow Indian Orphanage. My name then was Linda Lakoe. I was the oldest of five daughters of Richard and Amelia Lakoe; all of us had been removed from the custody of our natural parents. I have met my natural mother briefly and have corresponded with my natural father, but I've never felt comfortable enough with either of them to inquire about the details of the trauma that destroyed our family.

My nearest sister, whom I call Jackie in this memoir, traveled with me through the Oklahoma Indian child-welfare system. The others were adopted independently by various families. We have gotten to know each other as adults, but we have not overcome our initial estrangement to function as a real family. The wounds our natural parents and subsequent foster homes and orphanages inflicted on us have not healed sufficiently to allow that.

Introduction

I've gotten to know my extended Chiricahua family, descendants of the great Apache chief Loco, somewhat better. Many of them still live near Fort Sill, Oklahoma, where the remnants of our tribe were transported, as prisoners of war, more than a century ago. From their information and my own dim memories of early childhood I have been able to piece together some of this painful history.

I remember fragments only: hugging and rocking my sobbing little sister in a dark closet for what seemed like hours, until her diaper leaked and the smell sickened us. Loud, angry voices beating me about the ears; belts and calloused hands beating me on the butt and back; a slap that knocked me into a steam radiator, scalding my arm.

The heart of our problem seems to have been the tension between Native American and white, traditional and modern, that divides so much of Indian country, family against family, father against son, brother against brother. My father's oldest brother was born during the long Chiricahua imprisonment in Florida; he was a traditionalist, a man of respect in the tribe. My father married outside the tribe, taking a Shoshone-Sioux bride he met in boarding school. He served in World War II and came to know the world beyond our home place. He changed the family name from Loco to Lakoe, reportedly in the belief that he could not earn the respect of his fellow soldiers as Sergeant Loco.

At war's end the Lakoes left Oklahoma. I was born in San Francisco. When my mother was carrying me, she chanced to meet the lovely actress Linda Darnell, who blessed her ample belly; hence my birth name, Linda. Whether the blessing had effect is open to question. It is true that I have performed on the stage, at school and in community theater, from time to time in my life; you will also read of less formal settings in which acting served me well. Perhaps that talent is a consequence of Linda Darnell's touch.

My parents returned to the Anadarko area in southwestern Oklahoma when their marriage began to collapse, but my father remained at odds with the traditional branch of the Loco family. As far as I know, he has lived most of his adult life in California.

Apparently, the extended family was aware of incidents of abuse and neglect; they have confirmed some of my very early, confused memories. As I understand it, their reluctance to intervene on our behalf, which reflects a delicacy typical of tribal people, led the Oklahoma child-welfare system to take us out of the family circle altogether.

The break-up was very painful. I remember when my baby sister was lifted from my thin arms when I was only four. She wailed as she disappeared into a strange car and drove out of my life. I cried too, heartbroken. It seems to me that the pain of that parting had a great deal to do with the resolution by all adults concerned that my other sister, Jackie, and I could never be separated. Anyone who wanted one of us would have to adopt both.

It was that stipulation, more than anything else, that accounted for the later history of Linda and Jackie Lakoe as we passed from orphanage to foster home, again and again, drifting east along the back roads of rural Oklahoma. I remember rare breaks in our clouds of gloom, instances of compassion and kindness and camaraderie. I remember more vividly the terrifying storms—hard labor supported by thin gruel, beatings with fist and cane, and, yes, sexual abuse. I remember protecting my little sister the best I could from callous mothers and fathers who took us in for the inadequate allowance paid by the state and then spent as little as they could on us. I'm not sure how we came to rest, at last, at the Murrow Indian Orphanage, located on the grounds of Bacone College in Muskogee, Oklahoma. The important thing is that after years of constant rejection and abuse the little Lakoe girls who arrived at Murrow were damaged and defiant.

I spent my ninth year at the Murrow Indian Orphanage. In some ways it was the most difficult year of my life; it was also the most important. Some of my memories of that year are still so potent, so painful, that I am only now beginning to acknowledge them. As the memories return to my consciousness, I begin to understand how crucial my year at Murrow was to my development as a person and as a Native American artist. I've done my best to write an accurate record of that year, but the memories are forty years old now, and they are intensely personal and subjective. I've recalled our talks as clearly as I am able.

They express the gist of the topics we discussed, in language as close to our own speech as I can manage; they do not pretend to be literal transcriptions of actual conversations.

Jackie and I were the only Apache children in an institution dominated by the tribes of northeastern Oklahoma—Cherokees, Osages, Delawares—as well as the more distant Kiowas. Not only were we friendless and isolated from the moment we stepped through the massive wooden doors of the three-story red brick dormitory; we were also the distrusted and despised daughters of a tribe that inspired fear even in this outpost of Indian country. We were victims of the crudest stereotypes, savages in a savage land. Everything in my brutalized childhood had prepared me to play that part, and I did play it—with effect and relish—from the moment I was ushered into my bare single room at Murrow.

In retrospect my year at Murrow seems longer than a year. It held more pain than a year should hold, also more promise. It was the year when I discovered the healing power of friendship. When I came to understand that no stereotype could contain me. When I first began to explore the rich beauties of my true Apache heritage. When I discovered a capacity for beauty in myself. When I found my family.

My Murrow memories recall an America that seems distant in spirit but is not distant in time, an America that remains alive in the hearts of Native Americans of my generation who endured the indignities of Indian education in the boarding schools and the orphanages that tried so hard to wean us from our languages and our cultures.

The pressures and prejudices that helped to shape us decades ago still lurk just below the surface of the American psyche. Fortunately, they are not the only influences that work powerfully on us. In the final analysis, my story is about a triumph, not of fear and ignorance, but of hope and understanding. That is why I share it with you.

PHOTO ALBUM

The old people were right about photographs: they do steal a little piece of your soul. I say that because there's one part of my life that was never photographed, and it's the time that lives most vividly in my mind.

I'm talking about the year I spent in the Murrow Indian Orphanage in Muskogee, Oklahoma. The only pictures they ever took there were group shots. You know the kind—brown children, hair cropped close in institutional bowl cuts, standing at attention in long lines, very straight lines. Yes, each of us was dressed in a military-style uniform. I'm glad they took those photos; they can cut that particular image right out of my brain. Whenever I see one of those, I burn it if I get the chance. To complete the ritual of forgetting, I send memories of those long, stifling afternoons right up in smoke.

But that's something you want to be careful about, killing memories. Memory is a precious thing. I've just turned a corner and found some of mine. The Murrow memories. It's like there was an attic in my brain filled with dusty forgotten photo albums until one day—and I don't know why—I stumbled on that album.

But I don't want to get hung up on the concept; these aren't real photos. They're memories as sharp and clear as photos. My theory is that the brain was the first camera. It took pictures and stored them long before there was a Matthew Brady or a Stieglitz. And then, you see, with the invention of the camera, our brains got lazy. Stopped taking pictures. We simply lost the knack.

But because no one ever took any Murrow Orphanage pictures except those trumped-up paramilitary shots, and because I was still quite young, well, my brain kept the knack. It took all sorts of pictures of life at Bacone. The ninth year of my life, the year when I found my name, my family, and my art, lives in those photos. The trick is for me to assemble them in some sort of order. Then we'll have the story of an Apache life, of my life—Okee-Chee in pictures.

PHOTO

1

THE BACONE CLOTHES LINE

To begin at the beginning: Sunrise. A line of girls in a long gray corridor. It may be a trick of the light, but each, dressed only in a slip or frayed undershirt, appears thin. The light streams in, golden, through the high, small window above and behind the vast oak cabinet. Our closet is framed in the fire of sunrise; it seems that the door opens into a brilliant tunnel. A crisp, bracing smell of soaps and cleansers issues from the cabinet, as if the bright passage led into a pine wood in morning.

I am first in line because I've struggled out of the embrace of sleep with the first crow of cocks this morning. I have an ambition, a hope that animates me. There is a dress I want to wear. It's pink. It arrived only two weeks ago, making it the newest item in the wardrobe of the second-floor girls. It has ruffles and a bow; to me it is Cinderella's ball dress, as wonderful as that. So far, Mrs. Alice B. Joseph, who dispenses our clothes in the morning, our meals three times a day, our discipline and medicine when she deems it necessary, has given the dress only to her special favorites. I am not one of those. Phyllis, who is my enemy, has worn it twice. But today I am first in line. And I have reason to hope that Mrs. Joseph is a fair woman. She's told me more times than I can count, "Linda, just meet me halfway. You'll find that I'm a fair woman." Well, here I am, first in line.

Mrs. Joseph looms above, as wooden as the clothes closet. Sunrise surrounds her in a nimbus of light; it could be that she's a Baptist angel, a cigar-store angel presiding over a lineup of cigar-store Indians, although that thought won't come to me for many years. All I know this day is that Mrs. Joseph does not appreciate fidgeting. And most often that's no problem; at sunrise it takes all our energy simply to maintain the vertical. But today my anticipation of the pink dress has me supercharged. I shift from left foot to right; I clasp my hands in front, behind, in front again. Joseph fixes me with her steel gray eyes. I summon all my self-control to hold myself at attention. But she senses that she can outwait me. The silence in that corridor becomes so intense that it seems you can hear the sun rising high in the clear blue Oklahoma sky. The line of girls scarcely breathes. A rooster crows, and the sheer unexpectedness of it makes me jump half out of my flimsy little shift. Mrs. Joseph's lips turn in just the barest suggestion of a smile. "Linda, you know I won't tolerate that fidgitin'. To the back of the line with you, girl."

"Oh, but Mrs. Joseph, please. I got up so early." I feel I must plead my case, though I know from experience that it can only make things worse.

"Another word from you, and you will get no clothes at all today, little missy." I can hardly credit that; it isn't Mrs. Joseph's style. But there's no doubt that the woman is not pleased.

I can't take any more chances today because today the couple is coming. That's what my sister Jackie and I were told in the dread privacy of Mrs. Joseph's office, where we, trembling miscreants, expected at the very least to taste lye soap for some real or imagined indiscretion whispered behind her back but overheard. Instead we were greeted with, "Well, girls, this is very good. We've found a couple that has a definite interest in two little Indian girls." She paused dramatically. "I even said the dread word, Apache, and that didn't discourage them. If you can make yourselves lovable—yes, lovable, Linda—we may be rid of you."

Well, lovable—that will be a challenge. But surely a pink dress with bows and ribbons, Cinderella's dress, would go a long way. Even Mrs. Joseph must be able to see that. So why is she torturing me with a prolonged tease this morning? One by one the little Indian girls ahead of me receive their day's ration of clothing, and still the pink dress stays in the closet. Is she putting me through some sort of test to see if I'm worthy? Will the dress, so much desired because so long withheld, be my reward after all?

Phyllis had not received her clothes yet. That would answer the question. My eyes burned into her back until it seemed that the birthmark directly between her shoulder blades must ignite. I would have fused her spine into an iron rod with the heat of my eyes if I could, and watched the jelly of her thin flesh quiver and shake on the immobile column of her back; I hated her that much. She was Kiowa, for one thing, an approved tribe at Murrow and at Bacone College, which surrounded our little orphanage.

I was Apache. People looked scared when they heard that. Even here, at the Murrow Indian Orphanage. I'm talking about the Indian staff at an Indian orphanage. They bought the whole Geronimo story, the crazed terror of the frontier. The thing was, there weren't many Apaches in northeastern Oklahoma. My people come from Anadarko, three hundred miles south and west. So at Murrow all they knew of Apaches was Geronimo, my sister, and me. And I guess my sister and I didn't give them much reason to discount the Geronimo legacy. By that I mean that we met expectations; at least I did.

With a look deep into my eyes, past my eyes, Mrs. Joseph hands the pink dress to Phyllis. "Take it, honey," I hear her say, "it's the Kiowa dress." I'm quite sure I didn't make a sound, but in my head there was a thunder of rage. I didn't hear what she said when she handed me the well-worn navy blue sailor suit that had once been the prized outfit belonging to the second-floor girls. Later Jackie told me she'd said something like, "We don't want to fool the people, honey. That never works out. You're not a pink, frilly dress kind of girl. You're Apache."

I don't remember the couple who came to visit Jackie and me. I didn't really pay them much attention. I knew with an absolute certainty that it wouldn't work out. And, of course, it didn't. That pink dress was my only chance; without it, the whole exercise was doomed. I withdrew into the deep, brooding funk that was the commonest weather of my soul. The couple made a fuss over little Jackie, who had perfected her "adorable" act, but they shied away from me. They knew my secret; I could see it in their eyes. Without the pink dress to distract them, they could just discern the rash that lurked under my skin, ready to erupt into weepy, running sores. They would have adopted Jackie in a minute if I hadn't been part of the package. But who wanted a sullen, sore-faced Apache in a worn-out old sailor suit? Not this couple; that was certain.

I thought about jumping Phyllis in her pink dress. The idea tasted good on my tongue. But I knew from bitter experience that such an indulgence would only earn me a beating from the ruling clique and the further punishment of a lonely night in the infirmary without dinner. So I mastered my anger until dark of night. Then I crept out of my bed, past the lone chair in the cell of solitude and silence where I slept, through the curtain that served as a door, down the damp, shadowy corridor, to the towering oak cabinet, now bathed in the thin silver of moonlight. Mrs. Joseph didn't bother to lock the clothes closet since no useful purpose could ever be served by one of us raiding it. On this night I served a useless purpose. I took the pink dress, the Kiowa dress, and slipped into the enclosed dark of a broom closet. I cut the dress into a tangle of pink ribbons and then left it in a neat pile, scissors placed prominently on top, in front of Phyllis's door. Then I returned to bed to sleep the sleep of the justified.

I know Mrs. Joseph never believed that Phyllis had done the deed, not even for a minute. I'm quite sure that she did suspect me. For many days afterward she looked at me with a new expression in her eyes. She never questioned me about it; indeed, she never so much as mentioned the pink Kiowa dress to any of the girls on the second floor. Of course, it's true that we didn't get any new dresses for a long time. But I like to think that the chief motive for her silence was this: she knew in her heart that I'd had the right to do what I had done.

PHOTO

2

OUR VERY LITTLE "BIG PLANET"

Earth and sky. That and nothing more. I lie on my back in the dust-dry gully whose sides of crumbling clay rise up just high enough to block my view of road and cars and college buildings. I know that a handful of my friends are hiding or romping or lying in cowboy-and-Indian ambush in the network of ravines that spiderweb this acre of arid wasteland we've named "Big Planet." But it's easy to forget their presence, to pretend I'm the only person alive, that Big Planet belongs to me alone. The sounds of their play don't penetrate the pool of silence that floods the gully bottom. I hear only the rustle of scurrying insects and the rush of my own blood in my ears. I see only the vast sweep of clouds in the blue sky and the flurry of tiny life before my eyes.

I'm fascinated by the struggles of a red ant that's blundered into the perfect funnel of an ant lion trap. Time and again, the tiny creature scurries up the steep sides of loose sand, only to slide back toward the central hole and the devouring jaws that await. I consider rescuing it, but I've been stung by red ants. Not at all pleasant, almost as painful as a wasp sting. So I just watch, until the drama bores me and I remember why I've come.

It isn't to hide myself, though I love to hide here, in the maze of Big Planet. It's an aspect of the freedom I feel in this place and no other. Here I can run without anyone saying no or ordering me back into line. Here I can leap chasms, taking what seem to me fearsome risks that are thrilling for just that reason. And best of all, here I can lose myself, becoming, as I often wish to be, invisible to all prying eyes. "No one can hide like Linda." Mrs. Joseph often said it, and all the bigger kids agreed. Some went so far as to call it Apache magic, although certainly they knew better. It was no more magic than the invisible deer who suddenly bolts from a brake. I was in just that perfect a harmony with this waste of weed and rain-runoff gullies that orphans generations before me had named Big Planet. I don't suppose that I was the first to love this hellish acre for its silences, the freedom of its convoluted spaces, and its wonderful hiding places.

But as I said, I didn't come this day to hide myself. I came to hide a doll. A doll was a precious commodity at the Murrow Indian Orphanage. Some of the girls who were dropped off by their families when times got tough were given dolls when parents or aunts visited. But it was an unusual enough happening that everyone noticed. The arrival of a new doll at Murrow was disturbingly like a fresh kill on the Serengeti. Predators gathered, waited for their moment, and moved in. Dolls seldom ended up with their intended owners; instead, a small clique of the biggest, toughest girls housed impressive collections under their beds. As soon as the couple who never saw me in the pink dress shyly and rather gravely handed me the secondhand Raggedy Ann in her brown paper wrapping, I felt the eyes of the young lionesses on me. I knew they were awaiting the chance to strike. And I knew the outcome was preordained: I would receive a beating as fair exchange for a worn little rag doll. It wasn't that they were tougher—I was Apache, after all—but they were bigger. And when it came to me, they always struck in packs. However careful I was, they would find a way to corner me out on the grounds, away from whatever protection Mrs. Joseph might offer, clutching the doll, which, however shabby she might be, was still mine. Of course I'd have her with me; I'd never leave her in the vulnerable emptiness of my unlockable room. Then I'd have to fight single-handed and one-handed as I held the dolly fast in my left. And if she chanced to rip in the heat of battle, her kapok stuffing blowing in the wind, that would only earn me a stiffer beating. I'd learned that already from bitter experience.

So the only solution was to hide her. And Big Planet, where I so often and so successfully hid myself, seemed to be the logical place. There were, however, obstacles to finding a successful hideaway in this desolate spot. For one thing, there were so few landmarks. The dirt shifted and crumbled underfoot; the ravines crisscrossed the barrens with a randomness that made them almost impossible to identify and remember; the scrubby weeds all looked alike. For another, the landscape changed with each rain. The torrential downpours that accompanied our weekly threat of a tornado sent boiling ropes of water cascading down every gully, ripping at the clay banks and torturing the troubled land.

I knew all that; I'd already been caught in a hard rain and had to scramble my way out of the flood. I knew that I'd probably lose Raggedy Ann in the act of hiding her. But I would a hundred times rather lose my doll to earth and flood than to my enemies and tormentors. If I buried her and lost her, I'd still own the memory of her. In the most important way, she'd still be mine. But if the doll were torn from my arms by the big Cherokee and Kiowa and Osage girls, I'd see their triumph in their eyes at every meal. I'd know they were playing with her, enjoying her, and she would become a constant source of pain for me. I'd lose all joy in her memory.

So I held Raggedy Ann in my arms, there in the dry gully, and sang to her, an old lullaby that I knew from somewhere before my conscious memory. I rocked her like I used to rock Jackie when she was small, singing in a soft voice that never escaped the dirt walls, and washed her with my tears. Then I found a big rock embedded in the cliff wall and carefully dug out a neat, smooth hole just above it. I wrapped Raggedy Ann in a fresh towel that I'd stolen from the kitchen—how soft it felt, almost like a new wool blanket—and put her in the hole. It would be so dark in there, and she'd be scared, but I'd come get her just as soon as I could.

"Yo, Linda, I know you're out here." It was Simon Whiteturkey, a Delaware boy, one of the very few I thought I might be able to trust. Simon was small for his age but wiry and very, very brave. He was someone the little kids looked to for protection. It was getting to be the same way with me—between the bullies and their victims in size, and kind of tough, I was a person the little kids came to with their troubles. I got into enough fights defending my little sister Jackie anyway, so if some other little kid asked me, why not? I don't think Simon had any such motive; he was the only Whiteturkey at Murrow. With him, it was a kind heart that made him do it.

I looked up and put my telltale dirty hands behind my back. "Watcha doing?" I knew the answer even as I asked.

"Hide 'n seek." It was our favorite game. There were so many great hiding places in Big Planet that it was a real challenge to find anyone. No one ever found me unless I wanted them to, I promise you that.

"Hey, let me be a tracker." It was a strange request. Not many girls played, and when we did we were hiders. But that had gotten so easy, there wasn't much fun in it. Tracking was different. Every sense had to be sharp; you couldn't miss anything. And you had to get into the skin of the kids you were after, think the way they thought. I'd done it before, but unofficially, not really as part of the game. But I followed along behind the boys, then ahead of the boys. And, even though it didn't count, I tracked down those hiders; I saw them, but they never saw me. I was damn good.

This time it would be for real. "How many hidin'?"

"Three."

"All boys?"

"Naw, Phyllis one of 'em. And the Timm brothers, Ralph and Harley."

"Where'd you look?" He answered with a sweeping gesture toward the road and the orphanage buildings. He'd eliminated the easy part; he'd discovered me when he'd begun to search the eroded moonscape of hills and gullies that gave Big Planet its character. Great. All the good part remained, and I plunged into it.

But plunged soundlessly. That was key: to move like the wind, quieter than the wind. And I could do that. Soon I came upon some broken clods of clay, scattered impressions in the dust. The Timm brothers were real Indians, as we liked to say, country-raised and very, very good at leaving Mother Earth just the way they found her. This trail, a little too obvious for them, had probably been laid by Phyllis. I followed, but whoever made the track hadn't had much use for straight lines. Then a little brown bird—I've never been much good at bird names—flew out of a gully not a hundred feet from me. I crept to the edge, using a degree of stealth that would have done my great-grandfather, who I should tell you was an Apache chief, Chief Loco, proud. I leaped into the gully, surprised to see the Timm brothers on my way down, and tagged the both of them before they knew what'd hit them.

To my surprise, Phyllis proved much more of a challenge. Simon hadn't found her. Our shadows were starting to stretch out on the ground, so we set the Timm boys after her. Bewildered, I began to walk the maze of gullies, hoping that luck would accomplish what seemed beyond my skill. And that was how it happened.

I was loping along the uneven gully floor, no longer worried about who won the game, when I turned a corner and almost ran into an enormous spiderweb. The thing that stopped me was the sight of the spider itself, as big as my fist, sitting squarely in the middle of its web. I've never seen anything like it, gleaming yellow and black, with an intricate pattern of red dots seeming to grin on its abdomen, hanging, as it seemed, in midair by nearly invisible threads of silk. Evidently, I wasn't the only one who'd blundered into its lair: dead bugs wrapped in neat bundles studded the empty air. I was horrified to see that one of the silk mummies contained the corpse of a small bird. This was one huge spider.

I stared at the beast; it stared back. I saw the tiny hairs on its legs; it must have seen my nose a hundred times over in its faceted eyes. Suddenly it seemed to leap at me. The spider was heavy, and the web was thin; it fell harmlessly to the ground, but I let out a cry and stumbled backward. Phyllis, who, it turned out, had been only one ravine away, was the first to find me. She held me in her arms as I struggled to control my tears before the boys came. By the time Simon got there, my eyes were dry and the spider had disappeared.

I wasn't able to get back to the Big Planet for a couple of days. In the interim, we had one of the savage storms that punish Oklahoma in the spring. My Raggedy Ann doll was gone from her hiding place, washed away by a torrent that had scooped my little hole into a cavern and dislodged the great rock that had been her bed. The spider was gone too, the mausoleum of its web washed away, its bird and insect trophies vanished. I cherished the memory of my doll; indeed, I flaunted it before the pack of bullies, smiling my joy at having kept a treasure from them. But I've never been able to shake loose from the memory of that spider; it haunts my dreams even to this day.

PHOTO

3

IN A FIELD OF HORSES

Grass tickles my nose and my cheeks. I am immersed in grass; my world has become nothing more than an intricate green net. When I focus just beyond my nose, the near stems become as solid as the bars on my window, the rest a blurred tangle. When I focus on a middle distance, it seems that I am enfolded in soft green velvet, while a neat little wooded glade stands nearby. I feel a deep vibration in the ground; the tufts of seed that top the grass begin to sway as if a rhythmic breath were passing through. Now a thunder fills the air, and the drumming that shakes the ground beats through my body. The horses are running! If they were to run over me, crushing me under their sharp hooves, I don't think I'd mind, they are so wonderful. But they don't run over me; I've chosen my spot well. They stop to graze, near enough so that I can see the strong columns of their legs towering over the grass, the sinews and muscles of their flanks, the might of their arched necks, their flaring nostrils, the velvet of their muzzles. Surely, there is nothing finer in the world.

Sometimes I broke the laws at Murrow. Maybe *sometimes* isn't the right word. But I always felt justified, and never more so than when I snuck through the small, hidden hole in the barbed-wire fence that guarded the horse pasture. "Now children, stay clear of those horses," Mrs. Joseph would warn us. "Some of them are kind of wild. Horses like that have sharp hooves. And they bite."

Her warning was sufficient for the others. But I was fascinated by horses, all the more so when I found that they weren't the docile, obedient creatures I'd seen on a very few movie screens. They were dangerous, as anything so swift and powerful should be; their glory was inseparable from their danger. I understood that long before I could frame the thought.

Some of my earliest memories are of horses. Not the flesh and blood mounts, eating grass and breathing fire, that made our pasture a scene of wonder. The horses I knew first were small, cool Chinese blue porcelains. My real mother—this is one of my few good memories of her—gave me a whole handful of them long ago. I remember the jumble of tiny blue ponies filling her hand at the end of a very long arm. Her face softened into a smile, a beautiful smile. I'm surprised, when I think of it, that she had such straight white teeth; my own teeth have never been very good.

I kept those horses through a succession of foster homes; I kept them while I lost everything else except my sister Jackie. And it was because of Jackie that I almost lost the horses. I used to show them to her; I even built her little corrals of stick in the dirt where we played. But one day she buried some in the yard to spite me (it was about something silly; I think she wanted my Popsicle after hers fell to the ground). From that time on, I knew I could trust no one with my horses and that I would have to hide the four I had left even from my sister. Maybe that's how I became such a good hider, keeping mama's little porcelain ponies from everyone. Probably that's so.

By the time we got to Murrow, Jackie had probably forgotten all about the porcelains. They were never very important to her. I don't think she understood how important they were to me; she never would have buried them if she had. Then again, maybe she understood perfectly. That's why I couldn't take the chance of ever showing them to her or anyone else at the orphanage. Somehow those little porcelain ponies had become a key to my identity. As long as I had them, rolled into my sock or in any of the twenty other hiding places that I still don't feel comfortable telling you about, I felt like my secret self was safe. Whatever anyone did to my body, or to that part of my person the world required me to show, couldn't really hurt me. Not so long as my secret self, the part of me that played with horses gleaming with the light of my mama's beautiful smile, was known to me alone.

I started coming to the pasture because of the porcelain horses. It was even more private than the Big Planet, though much less free because the menace of the horses made me keep a very low profile. It's true that the big boys at our orphanage worked the farmer's field. Sometimes they caught me hiding in the tall grass or in the shade of a road apple tree, and they'd order me out. They might even chuck the heavy road apples after me, but I think they made sure to miss. Pretty soon it got so I knew their pattern well enough that we never got in one another's way.

The pasture seemed a perfect place to play with my ponies. I knew nothing about real horses except for the warning Mrs. Joseph had given us about these half-wild mustangs and the wonderful tricks I'd seen Roy Rogers's horse, Trigger, and Hopalong Cassidy's white stallion perform on the TV.

So I found myself somewhat in the position of long-ago Apaches when the strange, magnificent creatures with their broad, strong backs and long, tireless legs first wandered out of old Mexico and began to raise clouds of dust on the plains. What were they, and what was their special magic? My ancestors asked those questions, and so did I. They could scarcely credit the idea that men rode on the backs of these fearsome beasts; indeed, they told tales of creatures somewhat like the centaurs of old Greece—horses that grew human heads and torsos from their backs. Of course, I knew that men rode horses, and I wanted desperately to do it myself, but I had no more idea how to go about it than my forebears did centuries ago.

I hoped that my little porcelain ponies held a magic that would teach me the secrets of horses. I tried all sorts of arrangements—pointing toward me or away; in squares, triangles, or circles; in little corrals made of sticks and supplied with bits of hay, apple, and sugar—in the hope that I could draw them to me, pet the warm, damp satin of their muzzles, feed them cubes of sugar out of my hand, and then, if all went very, very well, grab a fistful of mane and vault onto their backs.

I never discovered the secret of their magic. The closest I came to sharing in their power was when the herd galloped, shaking the ground and beating my heart like a drum. There was a magnificent black mare with a blaze star on her forehead that I especially fancied. I studied her movement as she went through her paces, trotting, cantering, galloping. I stared so hard that I could see the moment when all four hooves lifted off the ground and she seemed to fly. I could feel myself on her back then, feel the thrill of speed as she raced in great, ground-eating strides. I shut my eyes and wrapped my hands about the grass stems as if they were the coarse hair of her mane, holding so tight that my hands began to ache, as the song of horse-speed shrilled in my ears.

But most days I simply lay on my back under a shadowy tent of grass, my little ponies parading on my chest and belly, as I watched the clouds pass overhead and listened to the bugling and thunder of the nearby horses. That was precisely the position I was in when someone nearly tripped over me one day, sending one of my blue porcelains careening into the grass. I scrambled to gather my ponies and hide them away before I picked up the girl who had sprawled face first into the grass. Oh, no! It was Phyllis.

"You okay?" she asked me. "I'm so sorry, I didn't mean to hurt—"

"I'm okay. You?" All the time I was eyeing her, trying to decide whether to kill her and make it look like the horses had done it. I knew she'd seen my little ponies, and she was the last one in the wide world I'd want to know my secret.

"Oh, I'll be fine." Too bad. "Ate a little dirt, though," she said, laughing, "and spread it pretty good on my blouse too. Good thing I'm not wearing that Kiowa dress. I'd get grief for that."

"Well, nobody's going to be wearing that." I couldn't keep the satisfaction out of my voice.

"I know. It's okee-doke by me," was her surprising reply. "Listen, I can't help being Kiowa. Any more than you can help being Apache. I came out here to talk to you, where no one else would be around."

"I don't come here to talk," I said. And then I didn't.

"I don't like bullies," she went on. "Although so many of the Cherokees and the Osages—yes, okay, the Kiowas—we seem to be the bullies. I like people who fight for what they think is right." She held out her hand. "My name is Phyllis Marie Goodbear."

16

I touched her fingers. "Linda Lakoe," I muttered, too taken aback to do anything else.

"You're wondering," she went on. "Yes, I did see. They're beautiful." She reached into her pocket and pulled out a pair of beaded hair combs, really lovely things, that I'd never seen in her hair. "My grandmother gave them to me," she whispered. "I always hide them. I don't trust those girls either." And before I knew it, Phyllis Marie Goodbear had disappeared under the fence.

PHOTO

4

SITTING THE STRAIGHT AND NARROW

The straight-backed oak benches are basketball-stadium long; the Bacone Southern Baptist Congregation is proud, prosperous, and very well housed. The church walls are newly whitewashed. The ceiling is tremendously high, and the windows are placed near the top so the light enters from the east windows in strong, straight diagonal shafts as if from heaven. The podium is placed so that one of the beams spotlights the pale, grey-haired minister just as he launches into his sermon, which is a very nice effect. We Murrow orphans walk the half-mile to church each Sunday in a neat paired line, then file in to the single long pew that will hold the girls and the one behind, which holds the boys. Each big girl is paired with a smaller charge, so that, viewed from behind, the pink bows pinned onto our neatly cut hair form what I will much later learn is a sine curve— up-down, up-down, all along the pew. The boys' crewcut heads form the same pattern. The minister is a white man, as are all the people in spiritual authority here, but the magnificent mural of Christ and his disciples directly behind was painted by the famed Cheyenne artist Richard West. So I don't mind staring straight ahead during the sermon; that mural is the most beautiful thing I've ever seen.

The wisdom of seating the boys behind the girls was lost on me. Although Mrs. Joseph, who sat as proud as a mother hen at the end of our row, believed that she had eyes circling her head, the boys managed to work secret mischiefs designed to get us girls into trouble. Ralph Whiteturkey was my favorite among all that bad lot, but whenever he sat behind me I found my bow untied or bits of a bird's nest in my hair. Once when Ralph had taken his place behind me, I felt a doodlebug attempting to dig its nest into my scalp. It caused me no little pain and the congregation no small commotion. Wearing the "I don't have the foggiest idea, so don't ask me" look that he was famous for, Ralph reached his hand in, pulled the offending bug out, and decapitated the critter on the spot. When we got home, I was punished for "not having the nerve to suffer a little for our Lord, who suffered so much for us." I didn't think it at all fair, but I will admit that Ralph toned down his hijinks after that.

On this particular day Ralph contented himself with pulling my hair, which I tolerated until he gave a pretty hard tug. I turned to glare so quickly that I hoped no one noticed, but of course I was wrong. Mrs. Joseph saw, and she gave us a look that I really think was directed more at Ralph than at me. It seemed that half the congregation saw as well. Our minister launched into a sermon on the original sin of disobedience, and I know that many heads turned my way.

"The first sin, the one that drove mankind out of Eden," he intoned in the deep, thrilling voice that filled the vast auditorium, "is the willful defiance of the express command of God. Do you imagine that God's creation is so meager that He cannot afford the loss of the fruit of a single tree? That God is a miser who hoards the goods of this world of His own creating? A jealous Father who keeps the tastiest morsels from His table, the fairest fruits of His orchards, the headiest wine from His vineyards, for His own selfish use?

"No. I tell you that God is the most generous of Fathers, who has said to his children, 'I will provide all the fruits of Paradise for your pleasure; you will know happy youth and perfect ease all the days of your life. And in turn I ask only one trivial obedience: you are forbidden to eat the fruit of a certain tree no different from the others. The knowledge of good and evil will come from your disobedience, not from its fruit.'"

None of this was new, and, for all the warnings about disobedience, I began to stir in my seat, perhaps hoping that Ralph would provide an excuse for my restlessness. "From disobedience comes the rejection of God. And that is the foundation of hell. Parents, you must obey the commandments given you by God and made vivid in the life of our Lord, Jesus Christ. Children, you must obey your parents." And orphans? Mrs. Joseph, I suppose. Again and again my attention wandered. I was a bad one.

"Let me tell you about hellfire, children. All of hell is paved with sulfur. Matches are made of sulfur. It is sulfur makes them leap into flame and pop and hiss and burn so hot. Imagine a world that is nothing but sulfur. The flowers are yellow, made of sulfur. They burn when you smell them. The butterflies are yellow; when they brush your skin, they burn you. The birds are all yellow like canaries. Yes, made of sulfur. You will wear yellow clothes that burn your skin every minute. That is hell. And that is where bad little boys and girls who cannot listen to their elders are sure to end up."

Now that last bit, that was not standard sermon. That was pure inspiration, and for a brief time it scared the hell out of us. It has occurred to me in later years to wonder what punishment is appropriate for a man who towers above an audience of children and uses his prominence to terrify them. But then I thought no such thing. I, we—all of us poor orphans—walked home silent, chastened, imagining what it might be like to be burned by birds and butterflies and flowers that flamed like matches and never went out.

The unappetizing Sunday sandwiches went pretty much uneaten that afternoon, but the milk and juice were never passed any faster, the apples and oranges never distributed more evenly, Mrs. Joseph's commands never obeyed with greater enthusiasm. We were a reformed bunch of orphans that Sunday; fear of hellfire had done wonders to alter our depraved characters.

At last Mrs. Joseph, who was kind-hearted, tired of our our "good behavior" and noticed our distress. "Sit down, children," she said, and we fell over ourselves in our haste to obey. "The Reverend Goodall was very graphic in his description of hell today, and I'm sure he meant well by it. Now, none of us want to suffer pain for all eternity, and most of us do our best to be good people and good Christians. But I am of the opinion that God is not as hard as all that on little children. I think He believes, as I do, that the gates of heaven fly open for the pure of heart and that the little children will be welcomed into His arms and enfolded into his bosom. Jesus loved the children more than anyone, and he advised all of us to be like you are. So I hope that you will not be afraid and that you will love one another."

I was relieved by Mrs. Joseph's words, and I've been grateful to her for saying them all the days of my life. But however comforting they were, they could not quite cancel out our fear of a place where the flowers and the clouds and the butterflies were made of match heads and burned forever.

Our cook had Sundays off, so both lunch and dinner were sandwiches of bologna and cheese on white bread, prepared by the big girls in our orphanage kitchen. Mrs. Joseph's reassurance didn't awaken our appetites much, and after an indifferent dinner, we moved to the big living room, where we enjoyed our Sunday-evening treat. Mrs. Joseph and the big girls turned on the TV to watch their favorites; we smaller girls found lines of sight that made at least a portion of the black-and-white picture visible.

For us, Sunday was church day and bad-food day and also TV day. The big box with the fuzzy picture had music, and girls and guys in beautiful clothes, and horses, circus performers, and joke tellers. Everything that our everyday lives lacked was in that box. I especially loved Liberace. With his sweeping pompadour and his blazing candlesticks and his elegant tuxedos and those plump fingers that ran up and down the keyboard, he seemed to me then the very picture of what they must have meant when they talked about angels. I knew that angels played harps, but I didn't really know what a harp was; I imagined that it was something like a piano. I could think of nothing that made more beautiful music than a piano with that elegant angel, Liberace, running his supple fingers with remarkable swiftness over the ivories.

We were fascinated by Liberace, as always. But Ed Sullivan didn't have much appeal this time; I think a team of acrobats from the Moscow Circus was the big excitement. I drifted away from the TV set. Some of the other girls did too. We were restless; I guess the minister's sermon was still with us.

Jackie followed along; Phyllis Goodbear and a friend of hers, Enid Wattanabe, a shy little girl also Kiowa; Rachel Waters, the heavyset Osage who reminded me of a toad and who had used her weight to hold me down in a fight more than once. I remember Eunice Cloud, Oto, who looked up to me in her quiet way because I did not receive beatings with the passivity of a wall as she did; there were one or two others as well, but they are faces only, not names.

"Oh, Sis, could there be such a place like the preacher said?" Jackie trembled and clutched my arm as she gave voice to the question on all our minds.

"I don't know, honey. He's a preacher."

"But Mrs. Joseph, she didn't seem to . . . I mean, she said that God loves us." Eunice had a hopeful look when she spoke, but it faded quickly when no one seemed to agree.

"Well, she's an Indian. What does she know? I mean, there are hardly any skins in heaven. Except for us Osages." Rachel glared a particularly hateful glare as she spoke, defying us to object to the ridiculous comment. Then she continued in the same vein. "You know why that is? It's because the only way to get to heaven is in a car. The rainbow is the road to heaven. And you got to get yourself a big old Chevy or, even better, a Caddy and drive on up to heaven when your time is come. The only ones who can afford cars like that is rich white folks and us Osages. That's because of the oil money. We got so many cars that when one of them breaks, we don't bother to get it fixed. We just push it away from the house and leave it."

"Oh yeah? Then where's the car to take you away from this place?" I shook my words and my fist in her ugly face. Rachel looked around and saw that her bully allies weren't in the room, so she got up and waddled off, tossing her head like an old English bulldog.

"That Rachel," Phyllis said with a sniff, "she thinks being Osage is about as good as being white. Maybe better. Her and her cars. Isn't that the stupidest thing ever? I don't think she knows one single thing about heaven. And if she knows anything about hell, I bet you she'll know a lot more after."

"You mean she'll end up there?" Enid seemed to know what Phyllis meant; I hadn't got it. "That's even worse than the matches. Hell will be filled up with people like Rachel."

That thought was enough to bring a curtain of silence down on our little circle. A world full of Rachels, and the flames probably not working any improvement on their characters—now, that was a vision of hell that would bring the waking sweats to the girls at the Murrow Orphanage. Enid began to whimper at the thought. Phyllis might have been her big cousin; I was never sure about that. She held Enid in her arms, rocking her and crooning softly.

"Maybe it isn't true," Phyllis said softly. "White men have never died and come back, any more than us Indians. Preachers don't know everything. My grandma knew a lot about the old ways, the Kiowa ways. She told me that our Kiowa beliefs were different. Real different. Nothing about apples and trees and paradise and all that stuff. Nothing about hellfire and damnation. Heaven, maybe something like heaven. The way she explained it was that between this life and the next there was a great deep canyon. Like, you know, you've seen pictures of the Grand Canyon. Like that, only so deep you couldn't see the bottom. Nobody knows what it looks like down there or even if there is a bottom. Anyway, there's just one way to cross the canyon. The trunk of a great big tree stretches across, the roots on our side, the branches on the other.

"Now when you die you want to get across because on the other side everything is wonderful. The prairie grass is tall and green. Herds of great, fat buffalo are everywhere. It rains every day in the summer, just for an hour, and then the sky is blue again. In the winter it gets just cold enough to put a skin of ice on the lakes and rivers. But the lodges are full of pemmican and dried meat, and pike and salmon come to our fishing holes and stick themselves on the spears. That's how she described it; I guess that's Eden for a Kiowa. What's more, your relatives who died before you are, most of them, waiting at the other side to make your crossing easy and to greet you.

"There's just one thing: if you've been real bad to anyone, or if you've been cruel to an animal or killed without the honor song, then that person or animal will try to make you fall right off the log. They'll jump out at you, or bite your heel, or pull at your dress. If you've been been bad enough to make them real strong, they'll twist the tree or pick it up and shake it, and down you'll go. But kids, even naughty children, they nearly always make it across that log. Their mamas come to the tree to carry them right across. That's what my grandma told me, and that's what I think is true."

23

PHOTO

5

A DIALOGUE IN TEARS AND LAUGHTER

White walls drain the color out of the light that streams through the big, high windows. No picture or calendar interrupts the white walls that wrap round and round me until I feel like a caterpillar imprisoned in the soft, white silk of its cocoon. There are six other beds in the room, all of them made military-style, their sheets crisply at attention, their corners neat and trim. In one corner stands a desk, in the other a table with straight-back wooden chairs. For Van Gogh the room would have been the material for art; for children it was a bleak and sterile promontory. I lie under a damp sheet, all alone. Only the progression of shadows marks the slow passage of time. As my feverish sickness subsides, panic takes its place. I'm all alone in the infirmary.

You might think hellfire and bologna go hand in hand. In some moods, I'd agree. But they didn't go together very well that night. I slept poorly, tossing and turning, and woke with the feeling that I'd swallowed burning sulfur in the yellow mustard on my bread. I stumbled through the curtain that served as my door and made my way to the bathroom—I won't go into detail; we've all been there.

The walls didn't reach the ceiling, so we often talked at night and had to rely on silence to keep our secrets. I wasn't silent that night, and I had no secrets. The second time I stumbled back from the bathroom, suffering at both ends,

Jackie whispered softly over the low wall. "Hey, Sis, what's going on there? You okay?"

"No, I got it bad," I managed to groan. "You gotta go get Joseph for me." Now Jackie was scared of Mrs. Joseph under any circumstances, and we both knew just how much the old lady loved to be awakened after midnight. I made my noisy way to the bathroom three times before Jackie discovered the courage to go shake the sleep from Mrs. Joseph. I know it was a hard thing for her to do, and I was proud of her.

Mrs. Joseph saw plenty of evidence of my distress in the hall and on the bathroom floor. I hadn't always made it all the way to the toilet on time. She was pretty good about these things; she had nurse in her blood, if not on a diploma. And she'd had plenty of experience with stomach flu sweeping through the orphanage floor. When you're one woman watching thirty girls aged seven to twelve and twenty more big girls in their teens, your greatest fear is the epidemics of cold and flu that run through the whole orphanage in a matter of days. She hustled me out of bed, away from all the other bedrooms, and into the closed white room that served as our infirmary. I'd been there before, of course—everyone had—but today I was alone. If this was some sort of plague disease, I was obviously the first to get it.

Mrs. Joseph washed me off and changed me. Her big reddened hands could be remarkably soft and loving. She made me take a big dose of pink Pepto and washed it down with a cup of hot tea. My stomach rejected her kindness, but she repeated the gesture, and this time it took. The tea warmed me; I was finally beginning to shake off the worst of my nausea. "Now you try to sleep, honey. And wait in bed until I come get you." She kissed me good night on the forehead and locked the door on her way out.

Mrs. Joseph was stingy with her kisses. This one was more healing than the tea and Pepto she'd administered. A warm glow spread down from my head and up from my tummy. When they met, I fell asleep. But I was by no means finished with my upset; I awoke a few hours later to find the thin silver light of a full moon pouring through a window and touching the smooth, white sheets of my empty companion beds with an eerie glow.

Loneliness and shadow can paint terrible pictures in a feverish imagination. They combined to terrify me that night. I began to see moon butterflies, pale creatures with soft white wings, flying in the moonbeam, then fluttering beyond the beam to alight on my walls. They were lovely and kind of comforting until the first one suddenly burst into flame. The others followed suit, one after the other, flaming out with the sizzling sound and intense white light of matches. They were the preacher's sulfur butterflies, and I began to wonder whether I might be in hell. A locked white room thick with burning butterflies was my first vision of hell until sunrise rescued me from my night terrors.

For some reason that I've never understood, Mrs. Joseph forgot that I was in the infirmary for almost the whole of a long, hungry, scary, and frustrating day. I thought then that she was angry with me because I'd been sick and awakened her in the middle of the night; now I suppose that she probably thought she'd dreamed the whole thing. I recovered my appetite by midmorning and was fiercely hungry and thirsty the rest of the day. I wanted to get up, but I was a little weak, and I swooned back into bed, head spinning. I took that as a sign that I'd better stay put until Mrs. Joseph came to feed me.

But I was afraid for Jackie. You see, we orphans weren't the only ones picked up by that school bus. There were a number of town kids who went to school in Muskogee with us. And we'd learned from bitter experience that they held all the power and respect in school. If they picked on us and we resisted, they would tell teachers whatever lie was convenient, and we would be punished. It sounds so impossible now, but that was exactly the way it was. Even if we arrived at school with a torn blouse and bloody nose, it didn't matter; we were the dirty Indians and we were at fault. That was that. No inquiry, no court of appeal. That attitude gave the town children a tremendous license that they didn't hesitate to use. They delighted in picking on Jackie, who was our youngest and had no fight in her. But I made it very clear that anyone who bothered her would deal with me and that I didn't care about punishments or beatings. I sat in a lot of dark closets in that school for my defiance. And I received beatings in that schoolyard; three, four of them at a time. But I always left my mark on them—a bloody nose, a bite, a black-and-blue shiner, something. They knew they couldn't torment my little sister without dealing with me. That was my pride.

Today they could; I wasn't there to protect her. The bus pulled away. I began to torture myself with thoughts of what was likely happening to Jackie. I knew all the cruel pranks of childhood well enough; it didn't require any exercise of the imagination. They would pull her hair, pinch and punch her, laugh at her, make her cry. She cried too easily; it made her a target. Lying helpless in my lonely bed, I bit my lip in anger and swore revenge.

It was a long day. My fears for Jackie subsided, erased by the sheer monotony of the empty hours. I began to notice the tiny sounds at the very edges of the silence. There was a cricket somewhere in the wall, under the window. Its song began to fill the silence just as a ticking clock can fill a large room. After a while, a second sound of silence joined the chorus. It was a sort of grinding. I looked very hard at the corner from which the sound came, knowing full well what I would see. I wasn't afraid of mice, and when this one finally showed itself, I was happy for the company. Although quite alone except for bedridden me, it advanced with a herky-jerky caution that was comical. Darting up, starting back, it took a most amusing quarter-hour to make its way the length of the wall. Apparently it had eaten whatever it had been crunching and was on its way to get more food. How I envied it; I even considered how I could catch and eat it but gave the idea up as impractical.

To my horror, the mouse made its way to where the cricket had been hiding, pounced, and silenced the insect with one bite, then scurried back to its hole. I could scarcely stand to hear the crunching now, and the silence that followed seemed frightful. My fantasies about Jackie became so graphic that I tried to wave them away. It seemed to me that our school was the place filled with people like Rachel, only worse. All flocking around Jackie, throwing lit matches at Jackie. My little Jackie was in hell, and I wasn't there to help her. I was alone in a silent white room; she was alone in a tumultuous white hell. We'd never been apart when it mattered before.

The hours crept by. At last the school bus pulled up in our yard. I ran to the window; Jackie looked alright—clean, clothes neat. What a relief! The only one who looked disheveled was Phyllis. I was starving for food and even more hungry for news. Every minute that I had to wait without hearing from Jackie was torture. Maybe this was what hell really was like; I couldn't imagine matches, even sulfur butterflies, being any more painful than this.

Finally, when sunset was painting the taut sheets of the infirmary sulfur yellow, Mrs. Joseph remembered me. She came in with a tray holding a glass of tea and a plate of toast. I looked at her, and a chill of weakness and frustration shook me. She looked at me and began to laugh. I don't know whether it was out of cruelty or embarrassment. Now I like to think it was the nervous laugh of embarrassment; then I ran past her, sending the toast flying, and changed into clothes in my room. At least I was free of my prison.

I found Jackie in the yard. I ran to her, and she jumped into my arms. "Oh, Sis," she said, "I was so scared. But Phyllis took care of me just like you would have. They started pickin' on me, pushing and pinching. And then Phyllis said, 'Hey stop that. Cut that out. Her sister isn't here. You're gonna hafta go through me.' And then she did. She fought them hard."

Phyllis smiled at me through puffy lips. I smiled back. I thought about the dress, the spider in the Big Planet, the horse pasture, and now, fighting for my sister. I didn't understand it all, but I knew I'd have to start thinking of Phyllis as my friend.

PHOTO

6

WILLING CO-CONSPIRATORS

Seen through the small rectangle of my window: the distant, three-story brick facade of the boys' dormitory. I don't see it very well now; my window is filled by the fair face and figure of Ruthie Tenkiller. Ruthie's one of the big girls—sixteen, I think—and she's the one I want to grow up looking like. Ruthie is a beauty. Her hair is long and black and lustrous. It reminds me of the magnificent tail of the black mare in our horse pasture, but Ruthie's is ever so much softer and finer. She has big black eyes and the kind of fine, slim nose you don't see much around here. She's not really allowed to wear lipstick, but she does sometimes. She's wearing lipstick tonight, though I know it's too far and too dark for her boyfriend to see. It's bright red, a color they would call sinful in church, but I think it looks wonderful. She stands in the window, fingers on my light switch, sending some sort of pattern of long and short flashes. Her teeth and eyes gleam in my darkened room. Across the way, on the third floor, second room from the left, her boyfriend sends a return message in Morse code.

You may have wondered why I've mentioned only one adult in this narrative. Surely, even someone as enormously competent as Mrs. Joseph could not have run the Murrow Indian Orphanage on her own. Yes and no. I mean, it never occurred to me to wonder about administrators and boards of governors. So, yes, as far as the day in, day out life went, and barring any medical emergencies, Mrs. Joseph was the adult in charge on the Murrow Orphanage grounds. But, no, she didn't do it alone. She had the help of our cook, Mrs. Treat, for one thing. And the big girls, the teenage girls who were wards of the state until their eighteenth birthday, did much of the real work. They made those awful Sunday meals, for one thing. They watched over us while we did our chores—making our beds, dusting the big staircase, watering the plants on the sun porch, washing the linoleum on the floor of that long second-floor corridor, taking the dry clothes off the line on hot afternoons. They hauled the dirty clothes to the laundromat on Saturdays and hung them out on the line. They planted and weeded our garden patch. They washed the dishes in our kitchen and at the college cafeteria. When we had visitors, they did the serving. They ironed all those clothes of ours and did the hard cleaning—toilets, stoves, sinks.

As I run down their chores, I feel like I'm writing up the list of Cinderella's housework. And, indeed, Cinderella was an orphan, just like Ruthie and her friends. The state could be every bit as unfeeling and cruel as any wicked stepmother. When I first heard that story, and it might have been Ruthie who read it to me, I thought of her as a Cinderella. Beautiful as she was, and worn down with work, yet so bright and bubbly with hope. There was one big difference: Ruthie didn't have any Prince Charming living in the neighborhood castle. All she had was Elmer Catches over in the dark brick boys' dormitory. Elmer was okay, I guess, but even Ruthie would admit that he was no Prince Charming. She thought he was the best available. I never heard her say any more about him than that, but I believe that she thought he was her ticket out.

The reason I know that much about secret, grown-up things between the big girls and boys has to do with the one job that the teenagers liked the least at Murrow. Each girl was appointed big sister to two of us little girls. Which meant they were supposed to look out for us—to keep us from falling if they could and bandage our scrapes if they couldn't. They were supposed to wipe our noses when we were sick, keep the strong from tormenting the weak, and hug us when the lonelies got hold of us so hard that we thought we'd dissolve in tears. Of course, Mrs. Joseph was too busy to check on how well they were doing all that. And they were teenage girls, all alone in the world, with troubles enough of their own to keep them more than occupied. So, for the most part, they didn't pay their "little sisters" as much mind as they were supposed to.

We did have one thing going for us, which explains why Ruthie was in my room that night. Our little girls' rooms were on the wing that faced the boys' dorm. So if our big sisters wanted to arrange secret meetings with Indian boyfriends, they had to sneak into our rooms after hours to do it. At one time or another, most of the big girls used their little sisters' rooms for just that purpose. They'd worked out a kind of Morse code with the boys, and our light switches were their telegraph keys. On some Friday and Saturday nights, rooms would be flashing light and dark all up and down the second-floor corridor. It was a sight to see. We little girls felt flattered, in a way, to be included in these very grown-up goings-on. Even if we didn't get along with our big sister, we never withheld our permission. And, believe me, we never ratted on anyone for their late-night indiscretions.

Now, don't get me wrong: for all the flirting and teasing and midnight message passing, Ruthie was a very proper young lady, as I remember it. She once told me that she believed in love enough not to confuse it with sex. Of course, she whispered that in the strictest confidence; *sex* was not a word we said out loud at Murrow.

When the time came that Ruthie wanted to use our room, she was especially good to us. An hour after dinner she gave us each half a Mounds bar. We didn't get candy very often, and the coconut and dark chocolate tasted wonderful. I hated to swallow, and I guess Jackie felt the same way, because a few minutes later Ruthie said, "Now, I'm not supposed to be bringin' you girls candy. Look at the mess you're makin'. You'll get me in trouble." And indeed Jackie had held all the candy in her mouth; dribbles of chocolate were running down her nightgown. Ruthie spent a good five minutes rubbing on the white nightie until all the stain was gone. She seemed very severe, but I heard her laughing about it with her friends later. After she got Jackie cleaned up, she sat each of us on her lap in

31

turn, unbound our hair, and brushed and brushed. That felt wonderful; living in the country as we did, our hair often got dirty and tangled. Getting our hair brushed was a real treat.

"Now, girls," Ruthie said when she finished with us, "I'm going to ask a very big favor. Elmer and me, we got to make some plans. And it's hard now they know we're stuck on each other. They make it tough for us to get together. So I've got to use your room; it's the only way I know. I'll be real grateful. You girls know I like you. You're like the little sisters I never had."

At the time I didn't have any qualms about helping her. Whatever Ruthie may really have felt about us, I knew I loved her like a sister. I mean, I admired her. I thought she was beautiful. I knew she was strong and brave. I bet that when she was my age, she was holy hell out on the grounds. She took grief from no one; Ruthie may be the only person I've ever known I can honestly say that about. So when she asked, I didn't think twice about my "sure."

Jackie snuck into my room fifteen minutes after lights out. We weren't used to staying up late, and it wasn't easy in the dark, quiet room. We didn't dare talk to each other or do any of the other things that might have kept us awake. We whispered about one thing and another, especially the day Jackie spent in school without me, and all the brave things Phyllis did to keep those town kids in line. That Phyllis, she was getting almost as high in my eyes as Ruthie.

About midnight a slim shadow slipped soundlessly past our curtain. Ruthie was wearing her white terry cloth robe, but her face was all made up with mascara and rouge and lipstick. I think she wanted Elmer to see her looking pretty from all that distance, and at night. Otherwise, I can't explain the Toulouse-Lautrec getup on a girl who usually had such excellent taste.

Ruthie seemed nervous. She brought in a bottle of coke and some paper cups and put them on the floor. I wasn't sure if she wanted us to pour ourselves a drink, but I didn't dare do it without some sort of permission. She rushed right to the window; by happy coincidence, our light switch was in easy reach. She flipped the switch to flash a series of light and dark dots and dashes; it was a weird and disorienting feeling to sit in our room while the lights flickered on and off, off and on. Apparently, Elmer understood the code, because he signed back to her. The earnest conversation with talking lights lasted a few minutes. When it was over, Ruthie looked happier than I'd seen her in a long time.

We sat down together, co-conspirators, and each savored a glass of cold coke. Now, please understand just what a treat a cold pop was for us. The only place you could get it was at the general store, a half-mile down the road. That place was strictly off-limits to us; and when we could talk someone older into bringing us back a store-bought drink, it was invariably warm. How Ruthie kept this cold remains a mystery to me to this day.

As she poured our cups of pop, Ruthie touched each of ours with hers. It was a gesture I didn't understand. "To a happy future for all of us," she whispered. "To love. To love. Oh, wish me luck, girls. I'm going to need it." I had no idea what she was talking about, but I whispered back, "Good luck, Ruthie." And Jackie echoed, "Good luck."

Ruthie shut off the room light. We drank our cokes in dark silence. When she stood up to go, Ruthie gave each of us a hug and a kiss on the forehead. A strange light shined in her eyes, though it was so dark in the room that neither Jackie nor I saw the red lipstick on our foreheads until we stood in the clothes line the next morning.

PHOTO

7

IN THE DEAD ZONE

The little pipe fence isn't high enough to divide one world from another, but it does. When I lie on my back, hidden from view by the tall grass and weeds that are no respecters of graveyards, the rusting pipe looms above my head. I know no one will step over it; in the times I've come here to hide no one ever has. Clumps of prairie grass consume the pipe here and there; directly beyond my feet some sort of vine spirals around it. The faded concrete markers surround me. I know the names and dates by heart. "Gladys Timm: 1911–1916 R.I.P." "Milton Denasha: 1899–1907 R.I.P." "Theresa Looking: 1904–1912 R.I.P." Eight in all and all very old, their simple messages nearly erased by the rain that represents the only tears shed over them. No living person ever brings them flowers or mourns them except me. They are all anonymous, and mysterious for that reason; but one is entirely erased, and that's the most mysterious of all. I gaze on that stone, as I often do, trying to make out even the shadow of its message, to retrieve some hint of identity. But I fail.

There is a comfort in the quiet of the grave, and that's why I've come. I wouldn't have put it that way then, but I did know that the graveyard was the one place on the Bacone grounds where nothing would intrude on my privacy. The horse pasture belonged to the horses; my heart beat to the rhythm of their hooves when I was there. Big Planet was full of surprises; I never knew what adventure

awaited around the next rise or in the near gully. But the graveyard first and
foremost was quiet. The spirits of the children buried here, if there were such
things, whispered in voices as soothing as the wind in the grass.

No one that I could ask knew anything about the long-dead children—who
they were or why they had been buried in that tiny plot of ground. Were they
orphans like me, claimed by some long-ago outbreak of smallpox or influenza?
Sometimes I liked to think so. I would try to imagine what life had been like here
half a century ago, before there were cars or schools or much of a town. Had
there been a Murrow Orphanage then? Or had this been some sort of reserve,
guarded by soldiers, like I'd seen in movies? I didn't know enough about my
own people even to ask the right questions. But I couldn't help wondering why
eight little Indians had died here so long ago.

Were they victims like me? Like me and the others, to be fair. We were all
victims here, except maybe Rachel and her friends. But nobody more than me, I
was pretty sure of that. I was the one who was always crossing lines I didn't even
know existed and getting holy hell beat out of me as my reward. It happened all
the time; it had just happened a couple of days before. I don't have this memory
whole now; some of the circumstances are buried too deep for me to retrieve.
But the pain of it is nearly as sharp now as it was that day in the graveyard, even
as sharp as the day it happened, in my school, just before lunch.

Let me preface this by saying that I had a tremendous bladder when I was a
schoolkid. I mean, I never went to the bathroom except at noon, when we all
went together. Which apparently is why I didn't know what I should have known
about whites and Indians and washrooms in Muskogee, Oklahoma, early 1950s.
I don't know what was different this day; I think my teacher had brought in
cookies and grape Kool-Aid, and I'd somehow contrived to get to the Kool-Aid
pitcher a couple of times. Anyway, come 11:30 I had to go to the washroom so
bad that I actually raised my hand and asked. There was a certain amount of the
witty give-and-take teachers delight in when they have a kid squirming in her
seat, but finally she wrote my hall pass and let me go. By that time I had tears
in my eyes. There was a girl's washroom right across the hall. It wasn't one I'd
ever used, but what the heck, it said "Girls."

35

When I left that room, the janitor was waiting to greet me. He was about fifty, with one of those noses just swollen enough to contain the explosion of little blood vessels that made it resemble a corsage of red and white carnations. I have a very sensitive nose myself, and I know I'd remember his smell if he walked into my room right now. I can't exactly describe it, but I've never forgotten it. Shine was part of it, the pungent smell of shine from one of the local stills. And that pine cleaner they used to clean out institutional washrooms. Sweat, his sweat, of course. The overpowering smell of this squinty-eyed, nasty little man greeted me as I came out the bathroom door. The truth is that I'd never paid him much attention before. I figured him to be one of the few people in my world who couldn't do me any harm. I figured wrong.

Without so much as a word, he grabbed me by the hair and slung me against the wall. A lightning bolt exploded in my head; through the wringing in my ears I heard him say something like, "What you doin' in that room anyhow? Don'tcha know nothin'? That room's not meant for your kind." My kind? I didn't know what he was talking about. I hardly had time to wonder. He dug his powerful hand into my thick, short hair and commenced to drag me down the hall. The pain blocked my sight, and I stumbled a couple of times, but I made sure not to fall. He would have dragged me down that long hall on my butt if I'd given him the chance. His fingers were still wrapped round my hair when he hauled me into the principal's office, but I guess that was okay with with the prim, fortyish woman in a gray suit who ran our school. "Found her comin' out of our bathroom. North bathroom, first floor. She used it, that's certain. So I'll commence to givin' it a scrubdown."

This wasn't the first time I'd been in the principal's office or confronted her face-to-face. But it was the first time I'd seen this particular look in her eyes. Sad, angry, appalled. She motioned for me to take a seat on the punishment bench, then reached for the phone. Her voice was so low that I could get no handle on the mystery from anything she was saying.

In about a half-hour Mrs. Joseph walked into the office. By this time a considerable knot had appeared over my right eye, and blood was drying on my lip. Mrs. Joseph gave me a look and went to talk with the principal. That is, the principal talked and Mrs. Joseph listened. One thing that I did make out was, "You know we do this over the protests of most of the town people. As a service to the state. Your children just have to understand the conditions under which we operate. . . . Now, it's a perfectly good washroom, and we'll speak no more on the matter."

Mrs. Joseph shushed my protest with a finger to her lips. She beat me about the head with her silence on the ride home; the quiet rang in my ears as painfully as the janitor's hair pull. She offered not a word or gesture of comfort or consolation, though I knew she'd taken in my wounds with her first glance.

When we got back to Murrow, she said only this to me before sending me to my room: "Wise people know the rules of the world they live in. When you follow those rules, the world isn't such a terrible place. Now, you should know that we're guests at the Rodgers School, and a lot of people don't want us there. They've set up some rules, and you just have to live by those rules. They don't want you drinking from the fountains where their town children drink. I guess they think brown is a disease you can catch from fountains. I don't know; I'm not defending. . . . I'm just telling you that if they kick you kids out of Rodgers, I don't know what we'll do. That school is promise for you, do you understand that? It's your only key to the future. So if they tell you to use just one bathroom, use that bathroom. Linda, Linda, you can't fight everything. You'll just end up looking like this." She cleaned me up with brown soap, a couple of Band-Aids, some iodine, and left me there. I was furious; I could hardly believe it. Mrs. Joseph didn't care what my story was. They were white and I was Indian, so they were right and I was wrong. I could never accept that. Did I have to go along with that to make my way in the world? Was that what she was trying to tell me?

That was the problem that had brought me to the cemetery. This was the place I came when I had something to puzzle out that needed absolute solitude. If anything, the spirits of the dead children helped me think. Sometimes I thought they whispered answers to me in the silence. It occurred to me to wonder if my problem was the same one that had brought some of them here. Could it be that Theresa and Gladys were Indians who couldn't accept Mrs. Joseph's wisdom?

Who chose not to eat the steady diet of scorn and abuse that must have been even worse sixty years ago? I tried to think of the humiliations they'd suffered. Cut your hair. Don't speak your language. Don't go anywhere without permission. Wear our clothes. I knew how they'd felt. They would have known how I felt when that janitor yanked me by the hair. And maybe they would have known how to take their revenge. They were real Indians, after all. Turn-of-the-century. Their parents or grandparents would have been free, known what freedom was. They might still have known how to use a bow or a tomahawk. They would have taken the scalp off that scabby old man; they'd have staked him out and split his belly open.

But no, that didn't seem right. That wasn't what I felt when I lay here, in their place, in the dead zone. I felt peace, even joy. Now, if I were buried here, my spirit would trouble the land; my anger would haunt the dreams of anyone bold or foolish enough to invade my space. These children weren't angry anymore; they'd gotten past their anger or forgotten it somehow. I didn't come here to fuel my anger, but to escape it for a time. They couldn't help me with my revenge; I'd have to work that out some other place, some other way.

In a strange way I felt grateful to the spirits of those long-dead children. I thought that since they were spirits of light, they should be able to see the sun. I began to pull the grass and weeds around some of the headstones. I cleared Milton and half of Gladys. Then I realized that the faded stone was the one that would need sunlight most. I don't know why, but a panic came over me; I had to clear that grave. I tore away the tough bluestem grass until my hands were raw. Then a new thought struck me: I realized that if I cleared the whole plot, I would lose my hideaway. I'd better stop this nonsense, leave well enough alone. I sat down and surveyed the damage. It was okay; the green screen was in place, but some of the graves were open to the sun.

The illegible tombstone had always been shrouded in shade. Now a shaft of sunlight fell directly on it. I swept away all the bits of leaf and grass that littered it and scraped off the patches of moss that had begun to grow in its damp, shadowy cracks. It seemed to me that if I looked hard enough, I would be able to make out the hidden writing. I brushed the worn concrete with my fingers to see if I could feel the imperceptible tracing of letters, and I stared as hard as I could. Suddenly I knew that the first letter on that weathered stone was an *R*.

A cold shiver swept through me, and my thoughts turned to Ruthie. Something was wrong with her; I could sense it. I hadn't really talked to her since the night she spent in my room flashing signals to her Elmer. There'd been something strange about that night, something disquieting. Ruthie. Ruthie had been so edgy, so hyper, and that wasn't like her. There'd been a kind of staring in her eyes; they'd been wider than eyes should be. She'd hesitated a couple of times as if she couldn't remember the code; yet I'm pretty sure that it was Ruthie who'd made up the code. And the gifts of pop and candy—they were nice, don't get me wrong, but it was almost as if they were too nice. As if she were trying to give us a message or something when she shared the coke with us and kissed us on the forehead.

It suddenly occurred to me that Ruthie was saying goodbye. As soon as I thought of it I knew I was right. I'd seen Ruthie several times since then, waved at her and tried to talk to her, but she'd seemed preoccupied; it was almost as if I weren't there. Her behavior had puzzled me, but now I understood it. She couldn't see me; she'd already said goodbye. Once you've said goodbye, there really isn't anything else to do or say.

But that left the question, Where could Ruthie possibly go? She was one of the older girls, yes, free to walk to the laundry, to the store, to the church, and about the Bacone grounds without special permission. But she certainly couldn't go to town without Mrs. Joseph's say-so. She didn't know how to drive, and she'd have to work probably a year to earn enough for a bus ticket. So just where could Ruthie go that would require a goodbye?

The *R* on that tombstone seemed like a warning. There were bad places you could go to—I knew that well enough. Surely nothing like that could be in store for my beautiful Ruthie. But the big world was full of mysteries and humiliations. As bad as the orphanage could be, the big white world could be that much worse. That was the thought that kept me from packing my meager belongings and running away after things like the washroom beating. Where was I to run to? Rodgers School? To that janitor? Or that principal? Mrs. Joseph could be hard as wood, cold as ice, but at least you knew where you stood with her. And to Ruthie, Mrs. Joseph wasn't really bad at all. I'd seen her twist the old lady around her little finger, as they say, on more than one occasion.

Then it came to me: Elmer. Elmer was at the heart of the matter, had to be. That was what all the frantic flashing was about. They'd made their plans that night, the day and time and all. Elmer knew how to drive, though he didn't have a car. It could be that he knew how to steal a car too. God only knew what trouble they could get into running off together. I'd heard whispers about a girl who'd done it once years ago and had come to a bad end. They'd sent the sheriff after her, the way I'd heard it. He'd used dogs, they said. Would they set dogs after Ruthie and Elmer? It was all too horrible.

I jumped up from the cemetery plot, didn't bother to pick the burrs and seeds from my clothes and hair. I ran the half-mile back to the orphanage. I would tell Mrs. Joseph my dread certainty, that Ruthie and Elmer were about to run away. She would put a stop to it, make them see their dreadful folly. She would shake sense into them or scare the foolishness out. She would . . .

Before I got home, I stopped running and caught my breath. I knew I couldn't say a word. The code wouldn't allow it. And the code was right. Ruthie and I were alike; our folly was all we had that we could call our own. I couldn't take that from her; I couldn't ask her to give it up. What she would do she would do, and that was all.

PHOTO
8

SOREFACE LAKOE

Eight tables filled with Indian boys and girls, big and little, in no particular
order, each with a tray of food and drink and silverware before them. Very little
conversation. The small ones are eating orphanage fashion, which means that
they're huddled over their plates, elbows encircling the trays like the rings of Saturn,
shoveling food as fast as they can. The bigger ones, the more secure ones, the ones
with powerful friends, sit restaurant style. Where a big kid sits next to a scared-
looking little kid, you know a lot of "sampling" is going on. The eighth table has
only one occupant. Me. I sit with my face to the wall, eating in solitude and silence.
I look thinner and smaller than usual. I know that, although I certainly can't see
myself reflected in the pale gray-green wall that faces me, just inches from my
nose. Let's say that I feel thinner and smaller and I'm quite sure I look the way
I feel.

It's happened again. I've broken out in running sores on my face, earning the
nickname I hate more than anything else at Murrow, Soreface Lakoe. I hear it
from nasty fools like Rachel and her circle. "Hey, look, it's Soreface Lakoe. Watch
out, you can catch that. Yes you can, you can catch ugly. Just ask her." Sure I've
heard it before. Lots of times. But that doesn't make it easier to take. The words
cut into my skin; I feel a new sore eating its way into my dermis, as if Rachel had
spit snake venom in my face.

There was nothing original about the name-calling. I'd been Soreface Lakoe since my third week at Murrow, when I had my first breakout here. Mrs. Joseph told me then that if my social worker had been honest and put my history of skin rash on my records, they'd never have taken me in at Murrow. But now that I was here, well, we'd all just make the best of it.

This time, I think it was the bruises from the beating the janitor gave me that kicked it off. Seems like instead of healing, they just got worse, started to spread, erupted into my rash. Although it could have been the injustice of the beating; when someone, especially some white one, messed me over that way, my anger wrote a protest on my face. It might have been something as simple as cemetery weeds infecting open cuts or as subtle as my worry about Ruthie making itself known on my skin. Probably the correct answer is "all of the above"; it often is on multiple-choice tests.

Anyway, we didn't worry much about causes anymore, Mrs. Joseph and I. We just did what we could to get the ugly thing cleared up. And part of the ritual "we'd" hit upon was that I eat dinner in isolation. As she explained it, this was for my benefit; it would cut down on the razzing and jeering, all the cruelty kids are capable of. And the simplest (yet assuredly the most humiliating) way of achieving isolation was for me to eat alone at my table, in the midst of the multitude, facing the wall. I'd a hundred times rather have eaten in my room. I'd have eaten under the porch, or not at all, if I could only have escaped that chair of shame facing the wall, in the midst of my enemies, with whispers of "Soreface Lakoe" washing at my neck and ears in relentless waves. But Mrs. Joseph seemed to think this was a trial of the heart, and I was reluctant to confirm her opinion that I was not only ugly but of low character. So I endured and bided my time.

In some ways isolation wasn't so bad. I didn't have to eat orphanage-style—I could relax with my food; nobody was going to help themselves to my mashed potatoes. I didn't miss the conversation much; I wasn't a talker at the table anyway. I didn't have to keep my eyes on Jackie's plate while Rachel robbed mine. Phyllis looked after Jackie now when I had my troubles, and I have to admit she did a good job of it. She was well liked, so that made it easy for her. One thing I've learned is that lots of things come easy for the Phyllises of the world, just as they come hard for people like me. That's because nothing stands by itself (except maybe me in that lunchroom). Things are tied together in chains; they stand or fall together. That felt like some sort of conspiracy when I first understood it back at Murrow; now I know it's simply the way it is.

My skin troubles made me a kind of project for Mrs. Joseph. She'd called a doctor in, and he'd made some kind of tests. "She'll always have it, incurable"—that was his verdict. Something about the way my nerves connected my gut and my skin. The volcano in my belly would erupt onto the skin of my face and arms and abdomen. There was nothing you could do about that. But by the same token, it meant that food might be key to controlling the problem. If you could find foods that untied the knots in my stomach, you might be able to heal my sores in just a few days.

For Mrs. Joseph I was a project, but she was a busy woman with many problems to solve, so she handed me off to someone whose talents more nearly suited my needs. Mrs. Treat ran our kitchen at the orphanage. Forty-something, tall, imposing, blond, she ruled over her kitchen with an authority and efficiency that was impressive, a passion for cleanliness that bordered on the fanatical. You could eat off her floors, and you would hardly mind doing it; her food was that good. She cooked hearty, healthy, satisfying breakfasts and dinners for seventy-five to a hundred of us, more when we were entertaining, yet she made it look easier than I can with a dinner for ten.

"Nutrition is a science," Mrs. Treat liked to say; she was very much ahead of her time in that perception. And the good woman had the soul of a scientist. I became her nutritional laboratory. For the most part, that worked out very well for me. Since the whole point was to soothe my stomach, we concentrated on foods that tasted good going down. Now, I had a lot of trouble with the powdered milk that was a favored beverage (because it was supplied in such copious quantities by the state) at Murrow. It was nasty stuff; I choked on it. Mrs. Treat improved the milk for me. She had an old hand beater that she used to whip up some of the most extraordinary concoctions: shakes of powdered milk flavored with strawberry or banana, peach, apricot, cucumber, carrot, piñon, prickly pear, ground pecan. Her ingenuity was boundless and startling. Her experiments could have been the starting point for a health-food and juice bar, except that such an idea was beyond the imagination of the fifties.

Most of Mrs. Treat's creations were treats. I loved the attention. I didn't realize how the special treatment was ostracizing me from the other orphans. What, did these silly girls envy me the pain and shame of my face? Apparently, incredibly, the answer was yes. When I emerged from a session with Mrs. Treat to find Rachel and three of her friends pushing Jackie around in a most provocative manner, I made no connection between the two kinds of attention. I simply accepted the challenge, clamped my teeth on Rachel's arm, and inflicted all the pain I could while I took my beating. It happened again and again, and it would continue to happen even after the treatments stopped; a pattern had been set.

Apparently Mrs. Treat, or perhaps it was Mrs. Joseph, was smarter than me about the group dynamics of orphan girls. They saw that whatever good the home remedies were doing was canceled by bruises from repeated beatings. The experiment couldn't work—not here at Murrow, which was such a woefully inadequate laboratory. But we had made some discoveries: bananas helped, oranges helped; unhappily, green vegetables also seemed to help. So I often came to the kitchen after the official meal for a helping of Mrs. Treat's delicious rice pudding, an extra orange or banana, or the biggest, ripest peach in summer. They were small things, but enough to underscore my special treatment, my isolation, my difference from the rest.

I was Apache, from an unknown tribe of fierce reputation. I was "Soreface Lakoe," victim of ugly skin but also the recipient of hotly resented special treatment. I was the toughest fighter, pound for pound, in the orphanage. I was silent and brooding and mean. I had few friends and wasn't likely to add many to that select company. But in many ways I was just like all the other Murrow girls. I knew without question what my favorite course in this humiliating meal would be: it would be dessert, and not the single dry cookie served in our dining room.

I'd taken advantage of my time away from the others to search rooms. I was particularly thorough in Rachel's room, my heart in my throat the whole time I went through it. Rachel was Osage and related to money in some distant way;

she always got the best packages from home. She hid them so well that she never had to do what the rest of us did—share our wealth before we lost it entirely. Instead, she would bring her treasures out before us, one at a time, and devour them with a thoroughness and relish that was pure torture to behold. I knew she'd just gotten a delivery, and I wanted it for myself. But if she caught me, there'd be more than her bulk on my back. Everybody stole, but no one was ever caught. And Rachel was maybe the only girl who'd rat on you if she caught you, though I'll swear she stole more than anyone else on the floor. Nobody could befriend a caught thief, not even Phyllis; that was one of the peculiarities of our code.

I found her hiding place. Rachel had a hollowed out space in her mattress, right at the foot in the middle, where she hid tins of home-baked cookies and cakes and heaps of fresh pecans in season. I opened the tin to a smell of chocolate chips so powerful that I almost swooned. I ate one cookie on the spot, thought about taking all the rest, then decided to help myself to just enough that she probably wouldn't notice. After all, now that I knew the location of her repository, I might be able to raid her cookie tin for months to come.

So when Rachel tripped into my table on the way out, knocking my peach onto the floor, I just smiled in her face. That must have thrown her, but her only answer was to hiss, "Soreface Lakoe." I had a better answer: Tonight, after lights out, I'd sneak over to Jackie's room. The two of us would huddle at the foot of her bed devouring Rachel's cookies. I'd chew them nice and slow, letting every chip dissolve on my tongue. Boy, they'd taste good. I'd hug Jackie, and she'd climb into my lap; we'd savor our little victory together.

PHOTO

9

A DILEMMA IN BLACK AND WHITE

Black and white are colors of night. Sitting on a fence just past the horse pasture, shadowed by the faint silver of a half-moon, a half-dozen young Indians gaze at pictures moving through the night. The tops of autos, all dark, huddle in long rows across the flat as if it were filled with the pupae of monarch butterflies. A great screen towers above the cars; the silent images of a Western movie flash across it. It's near enough so the horses and men and milling throngs of cattle can be clearly seen. But all the furious sounds of gunfire and stampede are swallowed by the still air. I don't understand how the cry of a nighthawk can be heard as it flashes across the screen, while the gunshots are silenced. Ruthie explains that the sound is conveyed through boxes that hook onto car windows, and we haven't paid our fare.

I'd heard them disappearing into the night many times, but I'd never been invited to come along myself before. It was a sort of mystery play, exclusive to weekends in the summer. The big girls would slip soundlessly up onto our floor, shake an exclusive group of designated little girls awake (most of us only pretended to be sleeping), help them dress, and slip out for some secret rendezvous. Mrs. Joseph knew all about the adventure, which took place with her blessing, but she played along with the secrecy, knowing how much drama it added for us. In fact, the condition attached to Mrs. Joseph's permission was that the big girls must take "little sisters" along on these outings. She was a shrewd one, was Mrs. Joseph.

46

I'd never been invited along, but I never gave up hope that someday I would be. My skin was beginning to clear; that is, the sores had stopped running and were capped by the hard scabs that always announced recovery. It may be that I looked my worst at this time, but the people who knew me knew that I was perfectly safe to associate with. Maybe that's why on this particular night the shuffling steps stopped before my curtain. I held my breath with excitement, waiting what seemed a terribly long time before the curtain parted and the slim figure of Ruthie slipped into my domicile as silent and weightless as a ghost. I started to speak; she clapped her hand over my mouth. "For tonight, you're a big girl, darling," she whispered. "And big girls know how to be very, very quiet."

"What's up?" I whispered even more softly than she.

"It's the big girls that are up, and off to the movies. And tonight I want you to come along. Now hurry, we've got to get some clothes on you."

I dressed in silence, too startled by it all to really think. It wasn't 'til I was halfway out into the corridor that I remembered to ask, "What about Jackie?"

"Jackie? Let her sleep, now. She's a baby."

"But she wakes up. Most every night. And if she doesn't find me here, she'll raise a terrible stink. She is a baby, you're right. She'll be bawling like a baby."

Ruthie looked at me hard, thought it over, then concluded, "I guess you're right about that. Maybe you best stay here. I'll just say . . ."

I think I started to whimper. I'm not sure; it certainly wasn't something I did very often. Ruthie shook her head. "Okay, get her ready. But if she wakes up Joseph, you're in trouble. Very, very deep." I think she was smiling when she said it.

It wasn't a particularly unusual thing for me to wake Jackie up in the middle of the night, so she didn't make much of a fuss. I didn't try to explain what was going on, just hustled her into her clothes. She was only about half awake through the process. It wasn't until we got outside, through a passageway I knew nothing about, that she woke up enough to ask me, "Sis, what are we doing out here?"

"I have no idea," I had to answer. I really didn't know what Ruthie could mean by "going to the movies."

We slipped back down the road by the horse pasture. The horses were out by some trees on the far side; they moved like shadows under the moonlight. Ruthie grabbed me by one hand and Jackie by the other. "The big girls and boys at Murrow have our own private movie theater," she said, being as mysterious as possible. I saw that we'd been joined by a half-dozen of the oldest Murrow girls. Eunice held Phyllis and Enid by her two hands; they were the only other little girls included in the select company tonight. We headed toward the pasture fence that defined the northern boundary of my world. I knew that it overlooked a big something—like an enormous TV screen without the set, or a giant movie screen without the theater. I'd puzzled over it before but never asked, and I wondered now if it might be our destination.

About halfway there we were joined by a rowdy group of Murrow boys. Ruthie dropped our hands and rushed over to Elmer, giving him a big kiss. I was astonished. I'd never seen anyone I knew do anything like that before. It was like she was singing a love song or something; the curve of her body and the smile on her lips looked like something I'd seen on the TV.

Now, don't misunderstand. Jackie and I had lived in a bunch of foster homes. We'd seen things—you bet we had. Some of those disgusting men, with their thick, calloused hands, had leered over our beds breathing their rancid beer breath on us. But everything I'd seen about men and women had been violent and ugly. I couldn't comprehend why Ruthie, who I'd always credited with good sense, would ever voluntarily have anything to do with boys. Now, as I saw her greet Elmer with a kiss, I thought I understood. The word *love* came to mind. So this was love.

When we got where we were headed, Jackie and I saw just what it was that brought our teenagers here on summer weekends. The big object that projected up in the middle of the valley was apparently some sort of screen. Black-and-white cattle with horns longer and sharper than any I'd ever seen stampeded across the screen, raising a cloud of gray dust. Now cowboys riding furiously on flat but very spirited horses waved their hats and charged soundlessly after the cows. From the horse's hooves to the top of the cowboy's hat must have been as high as the roof of our girls' dorm. It was amazing, like watching huge Trojan horses strutting and prancing for our pleasure. I was entranced—I'd never seen anything so wonderful.

I've never been sure what movie it was; you just couldn't make any sense of it. My guess is *Red River*—I seem to remember John Wayne—but when I watch that movie now it doesn't quite fit my memory. Anyway, it doesn't really matter what movie it was; we arrived after it started, there was no sound, and the plot was impossible to follow. For all that, what we had was more than enough to entertain—a tumult of ghostly images on a giant screen, the small dramas playing out in several of the cars, the frolic and talk of our own Indian teens.

I was mesmerized by the screen and for quite some time paid no attention to all the rest. I'd always ached to know what it felt like to ride a horse. And though I'd seen Westerns before, this was different. The giant screen seemed to pull me in. I could feel the rush of hot wind as horse and rider raced over the mesa kicking up clods of dry clay. My stomach tightened as the pair plunged down a steep hillside: back legs bent, neck arched, nostrils flared, eyes bulging. Then they leaped a ravine, and the following horses leaped—shot from above and below, backs and bellies soaring, legs tightening like springs, then releasing. I was with them in the exultation of their flight, my knees digging reflexively into the fence post they straddled, my hands flailing air as I reached for rein, for handful of wind-whipped mane. I went with the last jumping horse, springing off the fence and flopping on my belly. Of course they laughed, but I didn't care; I'd jumped a horse, and I knew I'd do it again. Nothing could be more wonderful.

"You're gonna hafta tie the little ones on Ruthie," Elmer laughed as he vaulted the fence to pick me up. "They fall asleep this late, and look what happens." He found me anything but sleepy and certainly not in need of any sort of rescue. I started dodging him, laughing and darting around like some half-crazed sprite; I was that excited and happy.

"Hey, you crazy? Get out of there with them horses. You'll stir em up, and then watch out." Apparently Simon Whiteturkey was one of the little boys who'd come out tonight; I hadn't noticed him before. But I could see the whites of his eyes now, glowing in the moonlight like coon eyes or rabbit eyes.

"You scared of horses?" I asked him as I resumed my seat on the fence.

"Nah. I got sense, is all," was his reply. "Them are mostly wild. And you see, they're wanderin' over this way."

"Well Linda's not scared of horses." This was from Phyllis. "Why, I'll have you know that—" I shook my fist at her; I didn't want anyone knowing about my secret visits to the horse pasture. I could see from her look that she understood me. "Well, she's just not afraid. I think she can talk their language, I really do."

We were distracted from our talk by Elmer, who laughed and pointed. "Hey, look," he said in a stage whispered for the benefit of the older kids, "that car's got the jumps. Somebody poured jumping beans in the gas tank." We followed his arm to a big old Buick station wagon that did seem to be jumping on its springs. I noticed a pair of Levi's rising and falling in the back seat. I didn't really know what was happening, but there was something almost irresistibly funny about the way that Buick was rocking on its springs.

The sight of it seemed to stir our teenagers, who commenced giggling. Elmer gave Ruthie a kiss and whispered something in her ear. She was not amused. Ruthie slapped him across the mouth, hard enough to split a lip. I thought it was hard enough to split the young couple up too, but events would soon prove me wrong.

The Buick door opened, a young fellow got out, tucked his shirt into his pants, ran his fingers through his hair, and walked over to the concession, where he bought an enormous box of popcorn and two big cokes. "Worked up an appetite," Elmer laughed. Well, that show was over.

I looked back up at the screen, but the camera had moved into a saloon, where cowboys were knocking down drinks. Then one of them pulled out a gun, and someone knocked him out with a bottle. Pretty soon, chairs were shattering on heads all over that bar. Pretty standard stuff.

"So you like horses, hey?" It was Simon, standing in front of me.

"Yeah," that seemed safe enough. "Yeah, I really do. I think they're beautiful."

"More than that." Phyllis must have really been impressed by what she saw in the horse pasture that day. "The horses like her. They come right up to her. I've seen it. It's like she charms 'em."

"You ever ridden a horse, then?" Simon was not about to be outdone so easily.

"No. No, never. But just now it felt like it. It felt wonderful."

"Well, I had a horse once," Simon went on. "My grandma had a whole herd, actually, and she let me ride one. A mare, a milk-white mare. She was a beauty—a jumper. But she could be sneaky; bit me once. I wouldn't trust no horse I didn't know."

I couldn't argue with that kind of expertise. And I had a new regard for Simon Whiteturkey. "There's a black out in that field. With a white star on her forehead. That's the horse I'd want, black as coal and shiny."

Simon didn't hesitate. "White's best, take it from me. You seen the Lone Ranger, right? Well, his horse, Silver, can do stuff no other horse ever could. Take it from me, what you want is a white horse."

So there it was, a question I'd never considered before. When I got my own horse, as I knew I would, should it be a white or a black? Once the question occurred to me, it seemed terribly important. White or black? I turned it over in my mind many times after that night, never guessing how fate would decide the answer.

PHOTO
10

THROUGH A VEIL OF TEARS

Ruthie's face. So close to mine that it fills my sight. So close that the outlines of her features blur, especially when seen through tears. She touches my hair, softly, gently, the electricity in her fingertips drawing strands of my hair up. She brushes my cheeks with her lips; her hot tears fall on my skin, calling forth my own. We are saying goodbye, not so much with words as with every gesture of our bodies. Somehow I know that the harder I hold on, the more surely I'm pushing her away. Finally it seems that in the dark, through my tears, I can see only her teeth, framed by an invisible smile. Her teeth glitter like wet stones in the moonlight. They grow smaller, then she turns her head, and, like turning off a light, her smile is gone.

I didn't imagine then that I would grow up to become the painter I am today. So I made no conscious effort to retain the memory of an effect that has haunted me ever after. The sight of a face glimpsed through water, as when you come up from a dive, and there, just above the surface, he looms, returning your gaze. Or when he's provoked you to tears and the shimmering blur in your eye transforms his mocking grin into a compassionate smile. There's something haunting about the radiant, intense color, the trembling dance of too-solid flesh.

That's the way I remember Ruthie — as I saw her that night, through tears in moonlight. I can close my eyes now, as I write this, and see her again as she was that night at the drive-in, the last time ever. I've tried to paint that picture, but it eludes me. Not a reflection on a pond, stirred by a breeze, but on the skin-thin salt pool that covers the cornea, stirred by a heartbeat. I paint many other things from those years, less important subjects, but my image of Ruthie remains mine alone.

I never guessed why Jackie and I had been brought along on this night of nights. Our evening at the movies had been such a merry melody that I hardly imagined it could end on a sour note. I didn't notice when Elmer disappeared. I really didn't pay him any mind when he returned carrying a big black trunk wrapped round and round with thick, knotted ropes.

The movie ended just then. When I think back, I realize how carefully timed the escapade was. Elmer's buddy, Jack Billy, materialized at the same time. Jack was a Comanche, so it was only natural that he was our top horse wrangler. He worked the pasture herd, where I'd often seen him roping and riding, pitching hay, and, from a distance, cooling down the mounts in the far barns. He was good; he had real command of the horses. Sometimes I'd see him racing bareback across the pasture on the black mare I so fancied. Bare to the waist himself, and bronzed, he was the perfect image of the Comanche riders who ruled the southern plains from horseback. This evening he was neither bare-backed nor mounted. He'd gotten hold of our old pickup, which he used to haul those heavy feed bags, and was ready to chauffeur Elmer and Ruthie who knew where.

As Ruthie made the rounds of her friends, shaking hands and sharing kisses and hugs, I suddenly knew what was happening. Ruthie wasn't just *planning* on leaving Murrow; she actually *was* leaving us, this very night. I thought about running back to alert Mrs. Joseph, but I'd never make it in time. How bitterly I regretted not having told her about my suspicions. Now I was going to lose Ruthie. How could I stand it?

When Ruthie hugged Phyllis and petted her hair, I was fiercely jealous. Then she picked up Jackie and gave her a hug and kiss. People were always hugging Jackie; nobody ever hugged me. This was all too much.

Ruthie came to me last. She held my hands in hers, held my eyes in hers. "Oh, Linda," she said, "this is the hard part, the part I'm dreading. There's nothing I'll miss so much at Murrow as you."

53

I just looked into her eyes. I thought I could tie a rope to her eyes with mine and bind her to the spot. It didn't work.

"Don't go, then," I said, and I was angry, punishing. "You don't hafta go. Mrs. Joseph loves you. You could be her helper. You could take her place in a couple years. Oh, Ruthie, don't go."

"Linda, Linda." Now she hugged me and buried her face in my shoulder. "You don't know how special you are."

I pushed her away. "Me? I ain't special. They all hate me here. I should go, if anybody. They treatin' you bad 'cause of me? Is that it? That why you want to go?"

Ruthie looked at me with surprise. "Oh, honey, no. Never think that. You're the bravest little girl I know. The only one I've ever thought to myself, I wish I was brave like her."

"Then why? Why this?"

"Maybe you'll understand some day. I love Elmer, see?" It was a question; she didn't like the answer she saw in my eyes. "You'll understand soon enough. Just listen, now. I love Elmer, and at Murrow they're makin' it real hard for us. Mrs. Joseph, she's forgot what love's all about. And you're right, if I stay here, maybe I will take her place. I'm afraid that I might turn into her, with a spine so straight and a heart of stone. I don't want to become Mrs. Joseph, honey. That's too much like dying."

I didn't understand. I didn't know what to say. I gave up trying to bind Ruthie with my eyes. I grabbed her with my arms, hard, and almost pulled her to the ground. She returned my hug.

Elmer didn't have patience for this. I heard him say from a distance, "C'mon Ruthie. No time for all this. The bus leaves at 12:30. If we miss that, we're in real trouble." Then he lifted Ruthie by the waist; I went along for the ride. "Finish up with the kid, already." He gave me a look that let me know he didn't think nearly as much of me as Ruthie did. I gave him a look that could have come from her daddy, if she'd had one. It said, "You aren't worth the hem on this girl's skirt. Take good care of her. If I ever hear that you done her wrong, I'll come after you with a lead pipe." Something like that.

54

Ruthie put her face close to mine and left me with the picture I've been trying to paint ever since. She left me with something else as well. "I wish I had a beautiful horse to give you. One that would ride with your herd. I have only this." And she slipped a plastic horse in my hand, a black stallion rearing and baring its teeth. "Think of me when you play with him," she said, smiling as she backed away, her teeth sparkling like stars in the night sky.

Then she turned away, but her teeth remained, a shining fixture in my night sky, a personal constellation that I named Ruthie. For a while we heard rumors about Ruthie and Elmer, tying them to all sorts of romantic and terrible destinies, depending on the nature of the teller. But I never saw or heard from her again. In time she became a figure of mystery, like the buried children, Theresa and Gladys and the rest, a principal resident in the expanding graveyard of one-time acquaintances from whom I'd become separated forever.

PHOTO

11

THE "FAMILY" PORTRAIT

These photos might still exist in someone's album, though I don't know why they should. They exist in my head, though I don't know why they should. Jackie and I are in the Big Planet, but we're not dressed for it. She wears a lacy little dress that looks like something for a doll; I'm in blue taffeta pants and a white blouse. We look dressed for a masquerade, and in a sense we are. We sit on the roots of a dead tree on either side of a sober, very fat middle-aged lady in a yellow and blue polka-dot dress from the Sears catalog. "Cheese," her husband says, and we all comply, though Jackie's smile is much brighter than mine. He's dressed in faded overalls and boots but wears a newly pressed white shirt and gaudy red suspenders. Husband and wife trade places for a second picture; Jackie and I don't move. We are auditioning for the role of daughters, but I feel that we're not destined to get the part.

The theory behind the visits was very simple. We were supposed to be so desperate for family that any attention, from any couple whatsoever, should make us perform like trained seals begging for fish. Jackie complied time after time, smiling, giggling, holding hands, perching on laps. She had a terrific act; I enjoyed watching it myself. It never got her a mackerel but was almost always good for at least an all-day sucker. And she had an adorable way of sitting with her ankles folded, her tongue traveling in circles round the lollipop, a smile on her lips, a tiny trickle running down the corner of her mouth to her chin. I enjoyed the act, but I couldn't do it myself.

I was something like the genie in the bottle in that Arabian Nights story, I guess; repeated disappointment didn't sit very well with me. The first time, the pink dress visit, had found me as hopeful as anyone. But by now I wasted none of that scarce commodity called hope on the process. I'd become expert at sizing up a couple, determining what their worst nightmare might be, and delivering exactly what was required. I must confess that it wasn't any great trick. In most cases, I myself—sore-faced, surly, fiercely independent, defiant, Apache—was already their worst nightmare. No Academy Award performance required.

Jackie and I were Siamese twins so far as adoption was concerned; we were joined at the hip by legal document. The condition under which our Apache family had surrendered us was that we could not be separated by the State of Oklahoma. Whether it be foster home, orphanage, or adoption, we must travel together. I don't know how many of the couples who visited us at Murrow might have taken Jackie with them if I hadn't been part of the package. Jackie believed that the number was considerable. "They wanted me, Linda," she'd say after an interview, or "It could have worked, if you'd only give it a try." She'd have gone with anyone; it didn't seem to matter how stern or sad or fanatical or simply pathetic they were. Or maybe she was just playing the lollipop game. I was never sure.

Before polka-dot dress and overalls came to visit, Jackie had me do her hair in pigtails and tie it up in ribbons. I put her into the lacy little dress that was the cutest one we had, did all the snaps and buttons just so. She was adorable, there was no denying it. I wasn't jealous or anything; I was proud of her, to tell the truth. I loved her, enough to let her go into the loving arms of a family, but the right family.

When she was all fixed up, she took me by the hands and said, "Linda. I want this bad. Please. Please don't mess this up for me."

"But Jackie, you haven't even met them. How do you know? I mean, they could be . . . terrible."

"I don't care about that. I don't. I want a mom and dad, is all. I don't care if they meet your standards. I don't."

I was taken aback; she'd never actually said it before. "You mean anybody is better than me?"

"You? You're not my mom. *I* can't even remember our mom; *you* can. I've never had a real mom. I want one. I want one. And if you'll just let me, I can. . . . Oh, Sis. Please."

That's why I was dressed up for this couple. I did it for Jackie. I had the bruises to prove I'd lay down my life for her, but I guess that wasn't enough. A seven-year-old needs a mom who's older than nine, a soft shoulder to bury her head in, not a bony little arm like mine. If they gave me half a chance, I'd go along this time. If they had any glitter at all, I'd be prepared to pronounce them gold.

Mrs. Joseph made the introductions, and I saw right away that there was no glitter at all. They were too old, for one thing; it looked like we'd be looking after them pretty quick. When "Mama" waddled up to meet us, she seemed to tip for a moment. "Papa" reached out his arm to steady her, but since they looked like a portrait of Jack Spratt and his wife, she sent him stumbling back into the mantle. It was like a comedy act to me; I couldn't help giggling. Mrs. Joseph silenced me with a finger to the lips topped by a very stern look. And Jackie—Jackie ran over to the man, who was rubbing his head, and hugged him around the legs. "You all right, mister?" I swear, she had tears in her voice. "I hope you didn't get hurt."

Well, the fat lady just about absorbed her in her great arms and bosom. "Oh you little darling," she said. "What a wonderful heart you have." She gave me a look that let me know just what her judgment about the merits of my heart might be. She fished about in a big straw picnic basket, pulled out a lollipop, checked to make sure that there was a second, and handed the big peppermint sucker to Jackie with the comment, "Sweets to the sweet." I knew then that if Jackie could have me kidnapped or killed, erased from the picture in some fashion, she would be well on the way to acquiring the mom and dad she so desperately wanted.

It was a cruel fate that bound us so inextricably. Even I, sore from a beating I'd received in defense of my little sister, had had cause to wish that we were free to pursue what were likely to be our very different destinies. But so long as I had to follow wherever Jackie might go, I reserved the right to dispense my hugs as I saw fit. So far, I hadn't seen fit, and today didn't seem likely to be an exception.

"We want to get to know you girls," the woman went on. It didn't seem that her husband was capable of speech; occasionally his lips parted, but no sound came out. "So we thought we'd have a picnic. We want to do the things you enjoy." She said the last directly to Jackie, who was sitting contentedly in her lap. "So you think for a minute and then tell me what you'd like to do today."

Jackie didn't take a minute; she began to spout almost immediately: "I think there's a carnival in town; I'd love to go to the carnival. And movies, can we go to a movie? We never get to. There's an ice cream parlor; I'd love a triple dip chocolate ice-cream cone." It was an explosion of greed that even startled me. I could see the man's eyes pop open; the woman looked like she would take back her lollipop if she could. Mrs. Joseph just shook her head and smiled. I'd always suspected she was on to Jackie; her look told me that I was right.

Jackie was quick to read people. She sensed that she'd gone too far, that her requests had exceeded whatever credit her hug might have earned. So she made the best recovery she could think of. "Before we do fun things," she said, batting her big brown eyes, "we always like to go to church and pray for God to bless the day. C'mon, the church is just down the road a piece."

Now, that was brilliant. The only problem was that I'd have to go along with it. Mrs. Joseph worked hard to keep a straight face, but "Mama" looked like she'd just had her prayers answered. A pious orphan—what else could a God-fearing prospective parent hope for? I thought about bolting right out of there but decided that I owed Jackie a little more support than that. At the same time, I made up my mind to sabotage the afternoon's proceedings. So maybe Jackie would have been better off if I'd run.

"Mama" took Jackie's hand and practically went skipping off down the road. "Papa" took the picnic basket in one hand and me in the other. "We could both run off," he whispered, "but we'd have two girls pretty mad at us." I liked him as soon as he said it, but I hated her. And I knew he'd be off at work or something most of the time, so what good would it do me if he felt like running from the same things I did?

They were impressed by the church, as well they should have been. Our Bacone Baptist congregation was likely way bigger than whatever wayside chapel they worshipped in. "Papa" walked slowly up to Dick West's wonderful altar painting and gave it a long, thoughtful look. "Mama" didn't seem to notice it, but she was wildly impressed by the lines of polished, oak pews. "Have you ever seen so much beautiful walnut, Papa?" she asked repeatedly. Apparently she wasn't much of an expert on wood. "Imagine the walnut grove that went to make this. Do you like walnuts, Jackie? How many of those yummy walnuts do you think these trees could have produced, Dad?"

"Not even one, dear. The benches are oak." He actually gave me a conspiratorial look as he said it. But it didn't seem to faze her in the least. She rambled on, proving she was an attentive listener at her minister's sermons. She led us in the Lord's Prayer. Jackie didn't actually know the Lord's Prayer; she wasn't any fonder of church than I was. I did know it by heart, so I kind of slid over real close to Jackie and recited it loudly. "Mama" kept her eyes closed in some sort of transport; of course, she assumed it was Jackie who declaimed, "Our Father, who art in Heaven . . ." Neither "Papa" nor I corrected her error.

By the time we'd finished walking to church and preparing ourselves to have some fun, there wasn't time enough to actually do anything. "Mama" and "Papa" lived almost an hour away, in a town called Claremore, which I'd never heard of then. They had to be back by blah-blah for blah-blah. What did it matter; we'd heard it all before. But they had packed a lovely picnic basket and wanted to share it with us. Was there any place here on the grounds where we could have a picnic?

Without hesitation I said, "The Big Planet." Since Jackie almost never went along with me, she didn't really know enough about it to protest. "Come on," I insisted, "this is real nice. It's the prettiest place at Murrow." I began to tug our heavy, hopeful "Mama" into the wilderness of Big Planet. She was wearing those thick, black heels that women of a certain age favor, and she found the going difficult. As we reached the dusty, rutted Big Planet, she began to lose her footing, lurching and stumbling on the unfamiliar ground. I knew she wanted to turn back, but she got no support from her husband, who seemed to be enjoying the spectacle nearly as much as I was.

I led them across one ravine and was eyeing another when I realized that she'd gone as far as she could go. So I headed for the trunk of a dead tree, and we sat down to have our lunch. I must admit that it was a good lunch. "Mama" had fixed some country-fried chicken with biscuits and potato salad and a home-baked deep-dish apple pie. The pitcher of lemonade had gotten warm, but it was still tangy and quite refreshing. I was partial to Mrs. Treat's cooking, but these were tasty dishes to set before two little orphan girls. Jackie ate and ate; she always had an appetite, and I could see that this meal had completely won her heart. She wanted this foolish, sentimental woman to be her mom, wanted it more than anything. And I knew from the tears making tracks down the layers of dust on "Mama's" overheated, over-rouged cheeks that she wouldn't accept me as a daughter at gunpoint.

"Papa" was having a good time, though, and in truth, our little picnic spot was private and picturesque. "Come on, Mama," he said. "Let's have something to remember the day by. Here, Jackie, you sit on this side, and Linda, sit over here." He took out an old box camera and began snapping pictures. Then he walked over to our log and took his wife's place. "Now, take some of me and the girls," he ordered, and she complied, though my guess is that hers didn't come out.

The ritual of the photos brought our afternoon together to an end. But as we were folding tablecloths and packing up the uneaten remains of the chicken and trimmings, "Mama" suddenly let out a scream. The giant spider of Big Planet (or a very near relative) had crept into the picnic basket, where it frightened her just as it had scared the bejabbers out of me. I don't see how I can be blamed for that; it never occurred to me that it would happen. But I know that Jackie did blame me, actually accusing me of putting it in there myself. As if I would ever touch that spider.

So it happened that this particular incarnation of "mama" and "papa" came into our lives on a sunny Saturday afternoon, taking photos of two overdressed little Apache girls with them as mementos of their experiment in Christian charity and leaving us unchanged. Well, not quite unchanged. I was confirmed in my cynicism about the whole process of interviewing parents. And Jackie was more certain than ever that she'd never be adopted so long as I remained the albatross around her neck. "Thanks a lot, Sis," was all she said to me. But she looked at me with hatred in her dark eyes. And soon enough I would taste the consequences of that hate.

PHOTO

12

THE WOLF PACK CLOSES IN

It's the view that a singular deer or musk ox, identical to the others save for the destiny that has separated it from the herd, enjoys at the last. Wolves circling—eyes gleaming, jaws slathering, teeth gnashing. There is no mercy in the pack, only bloodlust. Just as there is no mercy in the pack of girls that circles me in the yard. I've been at the center of such circles before, and they have tried my mettle many times. I know what I will do, and they know it too. I will single out one of them, as they have singled me out, and attack her with all my fury—fists, nails, and teeth. Rachel, leering and laughing at me, will be every inch as bruised and bloody as I.

I'd been raiding Rachel's cupboard for weeks now. And for the legion of the righteous who maintain that crime doesn't pay, I can only tell you that the Rice Krispie snacks, the pecans, the peanut-butter cookies, and the fudge brownies I liberated from the big tin hidden in Rachel's mattress provided the chief pleasures Jackie and I enjoyed that summer. Rachel never so much as uttered one word of complaint that came back to me. It may be that in the continuing orgy of her own eating she never noticed the relatively few goodies we reserved for our enjoyment. More likely, she noticed sure enough but decided not to damage her reputation by telling anyone about it. In a way, she was trapped by her image. After all, what kind of bully lets herself be victimized that way?

I knew that Rachel couldn't go to anyone with her problem. But I also knew that if I hadn't fooled her, she'd try to right the situation herself. If she ever got the goods on me, I'd know about it when her gang cornered me, and not a moment before. I figured she'd likely put some sort of watch on her room; sometimes I even thought I saw eyes peeping out from behind curtains. But no one was cannier than I, and I had no trouble eluding her guard.

The fact that she never changed her hiding place argued against her having caught on. Maybe, in her greed, she had never bothered to keep a record of her treasures; maybe she couldn't stop stuffing the goodies in her mouth long enough to count. On the other hand, there was the barest possibility that she was leading me on, encouraging my crimes until she had the evidence she needed to nail me. But that supposition credited Rachel with an astonishing degree of cunning and craft. I'd never found those qualities to be among her outstanding vices; she was far too direct and uncomplicated a villainess for that.

I discovered my mistake one late afternoon in high summer when I heard a siren crying "Sis! Sis, help!" in Jackie's unmistakable voice. Picking on Jackie was the bullies' way of summoning me. And when I looked around the corner, I saw that a crowd of my least favorite people, led by Rachel, had surrounded my little sister. They were pushing her from one point on the circle to another. Not hard—their business this afternoon wasn't with Jackie but with me.

My first thought was, Rachel's on to me and this is her way of getting revenge. I had to admire the way she'd found a place and time that virtually assured there would be no adult interference. The thought even flashed through my mind that maybe this time I had it coming.

Those notions were incidental at best; mostly I was boiling mad. Whenever anybody messed with Jackie, rage just took hold of me; I couldn't control myself. I know that Phyllis grabbed my arm and said, "Let me stand with you." But I didn't take any time to consider her offer. "My fight," was my answer, and I stormed into that circle of enemies. Very quickly they ushered Jackie to the outside. She had a smile on her lips that I didn't understand.

Rachel returned Jackie's smile. I didn't have time to wonder about that, but it did worry me. Golly, that Rachel was a big one. She weighed as much as at least two of me. And in these tight quarters my considerable edge in quickness wouldn't do me much good. I needed a little more room. So I bared my teeth and lashed out with my long nails. I'd picked up some big rocks in the yard, and I brandished them, threatening to throw. I did have one advantage over a deer encircled by wolves: I was the fiercest one in the yard.

Some of the girls backed off; their line wavered, and Rachel hesitated, so I struck. I hit Rachel with all my might in her ample gut, knocking the wind out of her. She staggered back; I lashed her face with my nails. I even got my teeth on her arm before her friends could react. But somebody smacked me on the back of the head with both fists, and I dropped to one knee. Then a couple of the bigger girls grabbed me and pinned my arms. I kicked their shins black and blue, but they held on, and the beating commenced.

I'm not going to go into a lot of detail. I don't really remember this particular beating all that well anyway. There's a kind of impersonality about beatings; one is pretty much like another. But I will say that Rachel's weight gave her slaps and punches a special authority. She could split lips and blacken eyes. She slapped me while the others held me down; slapped me again and again. She went after my mouth. Maybe she wanted to make it hard for me to chew cookies. I don't know; she never really confided in me about it.

There was a rule that governed our fights: when the vanquished couldn't stand up any longer the fight was over. Lots of girls would collapse to their knees, bawling to beat the band, after just a few punches. It was a point of pride with me that I didn't take a fall, but I couldn't keep vertical very long under the weight of Rachel's attack. We had a lot of fights at Murrow, but there was something vicious and mean-spirited about this one. I heard some of the little girls moaning and sobbing in the background. When I sank to my knees, the girls pinning my arms let me drop. I looked at Rachel through puffy eyes and saw that she had big scratches on both cheeks and a swelling contusion on her arm. There was some satisfaction in that.

"That'll learn ya, rotten little Apache. What's mine is mine; don't nobody never forget that." She spoke to the assembled throng of little orphan girls, not just to me.

Rachel and her friends melted into the shadows. The whole thing had lasted just a few minutes. I was on my knees in the dust, my left eye swelling, blood dribbling from the corner of my mouth. It was a familiar pose at the end of one of my fights. Jackie and Eunice Cloud were my cleanup crew; I usually limped off, using their shoulders as crutches. But today I couldn't locate Jackie, which scared me more than the severe pain in my jaw. Phyllis took Jackie's place, lending me a strong shoulder to support my wobbly legs. Eunice guided us through a seldom-used door to the first-floor washroom, where Rachel's friends were busy patching up their wounded warrior. Our two groups ignored each other. Eunice was a born nurse; she had a wonderful touch as she cleaned my wounds and chilled the swelling with cold running water. Phyllis wasn't much good as a nurse, but she did have the nerve to steal over to our clothes closet and procure a new outfit to replace my torn, bloody shirt and pants.

"I'll just bury these, don't worry," she reassured me.

"Okay, great," I said. "But I'm not really worried about Joseph finding these. She knows I fight. I am worried about Jackie. Where is she? I'd really like to find her."

Phyllis took the hint. The next time I saw her, she had Jackie in tow. My little sister was somewhat mussed up, but she didn't have even the smallest scratch or bruise on her. I checked that first thing. She looked me up and down and seemed furtive and a little guilty when she saw how bad my cuts and bruises were.

"Ah, Sis," she said, almost bursting into tears, "I didn't think they'd do anything like this, honest." Jackie had a way about her, an act she liked to put on when she thought she'd been caught at something bad and might end up in trouble. And that look, that all too familiar act, was what I thought I saw when I looked her in the eyes.

"What's going on? Where were you?" My voice was harder than I had intended. It surprised me.

Suddenly she looked evasive. "I don't even know what I did. They were just at me. And then . . . and then they started on you. I got scared."

My big-sister instincts took over. I held her in my arms and rocked her, crooning that old lullaby whose words I couldn't remember. "It'll be all right," I reassured her. "I think Rachel just found out about our swiping her cookies, is all. Now she's evened the score, she'll forget about it. Go back to just being the rotten old hag she's always been."

Jackie pushed me away. She gave me a look that wasn't one of the little-sister looks I recognized. "Linda, I begged you to be good. I liked that woman's cooking. She was real nice; I wanted her to be my mom. And you took her out to that awful, spidery Big Planet. I hate you for that." She stopped and looked at me to see if I was getting it. I wasn't. She ducked out of my hug and slipped away. "You bet Rachel found out," she whispered. "I told her."

Somehow her taunting words got into every one of my wounds and bruises and made them ache.

PHOTO

13

TO SLEEP, PERCHANCE TO DREAM

The sound of breathing: rasping, gasping, wet by tears. The night is lit by lightnings, its curtain of black torn by fierce winds. The curtain parts to reveal the faces of children—rain-streaked, grim, determined, etched with hatred and pain. I am one of those children. We all wear heavy boots. We surround a man who crouches on all fours in the center of our circle, head down, shirt ripped to wet shreds. One by one, we walk up to him. I kick wildly; he sinks down into the mud and groans. I hate him, so that I want to strike again, but someone else has already taken my place. An older girl leads us away; the biggest boys, heavy branches and rocks in hand, finish the deed. A final bolt illuminates the face of our victim; it's the school janitor who dragged me by the hair.

The dream was upon me again. I've had this same dream, variations of it, for as long as I can remember. Some things are constant: it is always a dark and stormy night; there are nine of us; we are enraged, on the hunt; we surround one man and bring him to the ground with sticks, rocks, fists, kicks; his breath is ragged; his face is always hidden until the very last moment. Some things always change: the face that I see at the last is rarely the same face; it is often the face of someone who has scared or angered me, but I awaken with the feeling that I have not seen the real face, that behind the mask of my current enemy someone monstrous and very real lurks.

The dream has always seemed terrifyingly real. When I awaken I am convinced that the thing has happened and that I've been part of it. Together with eight other children, I have beaten a man to death; that seems certain. But later, after I've calmed, after morning light has begun to warm the corners of my little cell, I'm not so sure. Then the whole thing takes on the evanescent character of dream: my co-conspirators fade into featureless phantoms; the villain becomes a hellish caricature, a Frankenstein monster; the night becomes a setting for melodrama or farce. I shake free of its grip, smile, laugh, play.

And then I have the dream again.

I had the dream years before we came to Murrow, long before I ever angered that janitor by blundering into his white bathroom. Somewhere in the long nightmare of indifference and callous cruelty, rejection and abuse that Jackie and I endured in our earliest years the dream arose to express my hurt and outrage and, in a strange way, to comfort me with the knowledge that abused innocence can hope to avenge itself. The dream came from younger days, and since it has burst into this narrative now, this may be the right time for me to share with you the shape of my first memories—the recurring patterns, the shrill sounds, the drab colors of my earliest years.

I remember father as a volcano of noise and temper, mother as a cold beauty who seemed always to be dressing to leave. I remember being entombed in locked, dark closets with infant Jackie for what seemed like many hours. Long enough to soil my panties and be scolded or even slapped for that when our parents finally returned.

We played, Jackie and I, in the dirt under our porch, snarling our hair with the seeds and burrs that blew all about in the scorching wind of summer. I remember the pain when those burrs were combed and yanked by impatient fingers from my tangled hair. Just beyond our house was a train track; it was close enough that the porch shook and the dust eddied when a train roared by. On the other side of the track were shanties thick with black children, who often spilled out onto the tracks in the exuberance of their play. Mother would take me by my thin shoulders and shake me; she'd point at the black kids and say, "Now, you must never play with them. Never. Don't ask me no questions; just do what I say." I used to wonder if those kids had some terrible sickness that made them the way they were.

From what I've been able to learn, Jackie and I were battlefields on which mom and dad fought their ceaseless war for dominance. Of course, I understood nothing of that then. We were plucked from that home by the state when I was five, Jackie just three, so my memory of life with the Lakoes is formless, a random sample of painful moments and the single loving episode of the porcelain horses. There is a very old scar on my arm, for instance, that seems to match a memory of being thrown or pushed into a hot radiator. I can't be sure, but there is a correspondence between memory and scar.

The State of Oklahoma redeemed only one pledge it made to Jackie and me—it kept us together. To do that, they had to make full use of the underbelly of our local child-welfare system. It wasn't easy, I suppose, to find foster homes willing to take in two wild little Apache girls who carried the official designation "difficult and challenging." They had to send us to homes that I now call "look-the-other-ways," places so cruel and exploitive that they could not have passed muster if the inspector had made even the most modest attempt to use her eyes and ears.

There were small dirt farms scattered around Oklahoma whose chief cash crop was orphan kids. They'd take in four or five at a time, send us off to school because the state monitored their compliance, and set us to work the rest of the time. I slopped hogs, baled hay, collected eggs from filthy henhouses, tended little garden patches, washed dishes in cold river water, drove cows and milked them—all the hard chores of the heartland, and I was only five, six, seven. Lots of places didn't have running water, I remember that; we fetched water in buckets from wells or even from rivers. Yes, we did drink river water—a comment on quality of life but also on the quality of air, water, land not so very many years ago.

Some of the hardscrabble farmers were kind, some not. Some fed us enough to keep us strong for work; some cut our rations to bare bones and tried to scare us into working beyond our strength. Some few hugged us and rocked us through our tears and tantrums. More cursed and beat us to silence our complaints.

The threat of beatings, backed by the memory of whippings with belts and green saplings, kept us silent when the ladies from the state came to ask their perfunctory questions about whether we got good treatment—proper food and clean living quarters. Why'd they have to ask when even their announced visits discovered thin, soiled pallets crumpled into the corners of squalid, overcrowded rooms? Why'd they ask, knowing that my honest, defiant answers would only earn me a fresh punishment? Did they care, any of them, really? Did they know how cruel it was to give me hope?

The dream visited me first in one of those dirt-floor, river-water little shacks. I've searched my mind and memory, and I nominate The Plantation as the source of my nightmare. The Plantation was a fifty-acre patch of bottomland planted in cotton. The graying, whitewashed plank house may have had a touch of grandeur once, but by the time Jackie and I arrived it had gone about halfway to rejoining the earth whence it came. The roof had caved in over a couple of rooms, which had subsequently been turned over to chickens and guinea fowl. Jackie and I joined the four kids already there, sleeping on mattresses scattered about our bunkhouse floor. The missus, as she liked to call herself, presided over the kitchen, which was amply supplied with cast-iron skillets and big wooden spoons—both of which were often put to uses other than culinary. She appeared ancient to us—probably about fifty—thick-waisted, red-haired, and-red faced, though both hair and face were spotted with gray. There was a memory of beauty about her; in other circumstances she might have been a Southern belle, a figure of charm and grace. But her life had turned her into a bitter caricature of Southern gentility, a woman of foul mouth and ferocious temper who demanded and received a grudging obedience from her little charges.

She fed us on pole beans, potatoes, squash, corn, and mustard greens that we grew in the ragged garden patch out back. For a treat, she'd flavor the greens with one of the chickens that scratched and fussed about the yard and supplied us with breakfast eggs. But she refused to cook up, or pen up, any of the four guinea hens that commanded the yard, strutting and pecking and making life miserable for all of us, kids and chickens alike.

Kids did the slave labor at The Plantation, planting and tending both the vegetable patch and the cotton fields. Only in fall, when it came time to harvest, did the missus find it necessary to hire wage labor. She relied on some of the migrants and vagrants who wandered Oklahoma's back roads to help pick her crops, putting them up in the dilapidated outbuildings that ringed the yard, feeding them stews and cornbread, and paying them with money she squeezed out of the monthly allotments the state paid her for keeping orphans.

I arrived in time to harvest the cotton crop. There's a knack to picking cotton, I discovered; if you don't do it right, stickers on the cotton bolls will prick your fingers and bloody your hands. But if I didn't fill my sack, the missus wouldn't fill my bowl with stew, and she'd throw my cornbread to those nasty guineas. So I picked my quota of cotton and slipped away in the evening to soothe my injured hands in the cool water of our little river.

I remember a very kind black lady who picked in the field with us, filling a much larger bag than the one I was tied to, looking at my hands one day. "You poor darling," she said, and she kissed my inflamed hands. I can't remember anyone, stranger or acquaintance, showing me such a spontaneous kindness before that moment. "Ain't no one ever showed you the trick in pickin' up these snowballs?" She proceeded to show me how to lift and twist the cotton boll without sticking my fingers. In time I got pretty good at it, and my hands healed. I learned something from her that would last: there had been nothing wrong with those kids who played on the other side of the tracks; the problem had been with my mother.

Some of the vagrants who walked the gravel roads, picking up a little spending money by doing odd jobs or harvesting crops, were decent men down on their luck; others were nasty degenerates. One of the latter came to haunt us at The Plantation. The thing I remember about him is that he had a red, runny eye and a sore on his neck that never healed. He was a "clean" man; often, when we were playing by the river, he came down to wash the dirt off, taking off the few rags he wore for clothes so quickly that sometimes we couldn't run off before he was naked. When that happened, he laughed his shrill, hysterical laugh or barked like a dog. Sometimes he'd do his barking when he walked past us in the field or in the yard. He was crazy; he scared all of us kids. We stuck together—worked together and played together—after he took up residence in our midst.

One of the girls, a little, frail child with a mop of blond curls, was especially frightened of him. He knew it and enjoyed it, calling out "curly top" at the top of his lungs whenever he saw her. It wasn't long before she was having nightmares and daytime shakes.

Something happened. I never really knew what, but whatever it was, it was bad. The girl was crying so no one could stop her, and then a car came by and drove her away. We never saw her again.

All us kids met down by the river to talk about it. We all hated him and believed that whatever had happened, he'd done it. The biggest boy, who was twelve and very brave and strong for his age, kept saying, "We can't let him get away with it. He'll do it again, to someone else, as long as he stays here." I never knew just what it was he was accused of, but I knew I hated him and feared him and wanted him out of my world.

I remember a dark night of fearful confusion, terror, and triumph. I know that the vagrant disappeared from The Plantation at that time; that he was never again mentioned in a voice above a whisper. Our brave young protector was moved to another home just a few days later, and Jackie and I were taken away right after the conclusion of the cotton harvest.

The dreams started some months after we left The Plantation. What happened in the dreams didn't scare me; if anything, the dream drama comforted and reassured. But the intense reality of my nightmares did frighten me. While I was in their grip, they seemed more real than anything that happened in my waking life. I was terrified that I would never escape the dream's strange, hallucinatory world of wind and lightning, of pursuit and horrible vengeance.

Another horror is the face that gazes at me in that last flash of lightning. It never has the telltale bloodshot eye or the putrid sore on the neck that are the only details of the vagrant's face I can recall. Most often, it is the face of a far more recent tormenter, but I fear that what I see is only a mask beneath which lurks the visage of my primal horror. When I see his image and recognize it, I'll know for certain that I participated in a great crime.

After Jackie's betrayal, the dream came to me once again at Murrow. Night after night it plagued me. Time and again I saw the janitor's face or Rachel's at the last, and both seemed fitting. But one night I saw something awful in my dream: Jackie's face—the face of my little sister, whom I loved better than my life—pleading with me at the end.

PHOTO

14

THE HORNS OF A DILEMMA

It is the first time I've ever appeared in a frame, either as a photo or portrait painting or as a living, breathing human being. My window is tall and narrow; when I stand up in it, after laboriously cranking open enough of a space to climb through, I find that I'm squeezed on the sides but have plenty of room overhead. The window ledge is no more than a few inches wide. Although I have good balance, I have great difficulty in keeping myself steady. Behind me is Murrow, which has become intolerable. It is a place of pain and nightmares and betrayal; it seems that whatever I do here turns out to be wrong. In front of me is a surprising emptiness: the big kids are at chores, and the little boys and girls are playing tag across the road, on the fringes of Big Planet. The grounds are open and peaceful. My room is crowded with nightmare memories of my recent misfortunes. I feel that I have to get away; the most pressing thing in the world is for me to just get away. So I step off the ledge. I'm wearing a little dress that has one of those black patent leather belts in the back. The belt catches on some sort of metal hook projecting from the window. It holds. I hang suspended between the blue sky and the hard, sun-baked ground two stories below.

You hear about the straw that broke the camel's back, and it seems like just another one of those clever sayings. But the thing that put me up on that window ledge really was a straw, nothing more. I was getting ready to go out with the kids and play tag on Big Planet, when Mrs. Joseph called me over. I almost ran off, but she was in that arms-folded-across-the-chest pose that commanded your attention, so I obeyed the summons.

"Linda," she said sternly, pausing after the name, which was never a good sign. "What was your chore for the day?"

She didn't usually forget the chore schedule, so I suspected something was up. But I couldn't see anything else to do but answer. "I was sweepin' the second floor hall, Mrs. Joseph."

"And do you think you did the kind of job we have a right to expect?"

I didn't like where this seemed to be going. "I didn't skip any corners this time. I covered that floor one end to the other."

"I'm sure you did, dear. But Linda, you have to look at what you're doing." Here she unfolded her arms and showed me a small handful of broom straws. "The broom was defective; it was shedding straw. Didn't you see that? There are straws all over that hallway."

Well, I knew that was a big exaggeration. Was she trying to tell me that I didn't know how to sweep a hall? Nobody had ever had cause to question my work before; I was always a good worker. And so many of the little girls were shirkers. Now, just because the broom was broken or something, I was being called to account for that? "If the broom was broke, I didn't see it. I was sweeping is what."

Mrs. Joseph shook her head. "Next time, do a good job. Now you go to your room and think about it."

She didn't have to ask me twice: I ran to my room. Hot tears of rage were gathering at the corners of my eyes. I didn't ever let anyone at Murrow see me cry. That was my credo. So I ran to my room before the tears could take hold of me.

When I got to my room, I felt hot. Hot from anger and frustration, and all the running, I guess. The room seemed hot too, insufferably hot. I went to the window to crank it open a crack, just to get some fresh air in, though I knew that the summer wind was hotter than the shadowy interior could possibly be.

While I was cranking, which was hard work because the hot metal had swelled until it didn't want to turn, I got the strange feeling that my room was filling with phantoms. The runaway Ruthie was there, looking mournful, as if one of the bad things everyone was always predicting for her had already happened. Mrs. Joseph was there, a stern and disapproving look on her face. That school janitor who'd slung me around was there, and the guy from The Plantation with the red, runny eyes too. The scary thing about them was that I couldn't really tell them apart. Could it be that the guy I dreamed we'd killed years ago had turned up at my school? Rachel was there, and the terrible thing was that she had Jackie in her arms; both of them were sticking their tongues out at me. The only ones who weren't there were Phyllis and Eunice and Mrs. Treat, my handful of friends at Murrow. My room belonged to my enemies; I was so sure of that, I didn't even bother to turn my head to confirm it. I only knew that I had to get away. Get away from all the hurt and humiliation, from the meanness and pettiness and cruelty that dogged me every day of my life. "Get away. Get away. Get away"—the words were beating like a drum in my brain.

The next thing I knew, I was standing on that window ledge. I didn't really think about what might happen. I just knew that everything I hated and feared was in my room and coming after me. Before me was a perfectly empty landscape, fusing at the far horizon with a cloudless sky. I took a single step off the window ledge.

Instantly I began my violent plunge toward the ground, cracking my head into the ancient brick of the Murrow Orphanage building, leaving a smear of Chiricahua Apache blood that may be there to this day. The smack on the head awakened me from my trance, leaving me in the astonishing position of someone balanced between life and death, between heaven and earth. For some utterly mystifying reason—one that was no less mystifying when I discovered it—I fell no further.

In my panic, I groped to discover what could be holding me in this unnatural position. I realized that a fall twenty feet to the hard ground below would shatter my bones, crippling me if it didn't kill. I knew for certain that I didn't want to be crippled, so if I were to fall, it would have to be fatally, headfirst. My hands discovered the hook that held me and the belt buckle that had somehow caught without snapping or pulling free.

I gripped the window ledge with both hands and, with surprising calm, took stock of my situation. Below, nearly at my feet, was the dead trunk of a great tree. It was far smaller than the mythical tree of Phyllis's story, but as I stared at it, my head throbbing, the trunk seemed to grow larger in my sight, until I began to think it might be that very tree. Perhaps, if I jumped on it, I would find the way out of my dilemma. After all, its far end was anchored in a heavenly place where everyone would love me. But no, it wasn't big enough for that; I didn't see any way I could jump and not fall off.

At the moment that thought occurred to me, I understood why the phantoms had gathered in my room. They were people I'd wronged somehow; they would grab at my legs and turn or tip the trunk to knock me off into the abyss. How close they had come to succeeding in their wicked purpose. I couldn't let them get the best of me; I must climb back up into my room, to life. And I knew with an absolute certainty that they wouldn't be there when I returned. Defeated in their wicked purpose, they would evaporate into whatever mist of the mind gave them refuge, lurking until my weakness and fear gave them another chance to get the best of me.

Once I made my decision for life and hope, the real horror began. Pulling myself back into that window was a whole lot easier said than done. I had to unhook the belt, but I couldn't lose my grip in the process. And I couldn't cry out for help, because I knew that trying to kill myself, as everyone would understand this, would probably land me in the nut house. Finally, inching around, I turned my body far enough so I could see the buckle that had become my lifeline. I flung my right arm onto the concrete ledge, getting the best grip I could, scraping my elbow in the process. I tried to pull the buckle off the hook, but all my weight held it on, so I had to give that up. I decided to unfasten the buckle, but to do that I had to push my body away from the brick with my feet. Sweat was pouring down my forehead and wetting my palms; I was terrified that I would lose my grip. At last I got the belt off; it fell to the ground—it instead of me.

Now it was a matter of hauling myself up, but after all my exertions, that was no easy trick. I pulled up and fell back, pulled up and fell back. I was almost ready to cry out for help, hang the consequences, when I heard a sound of laughter in my room. The phantoms lurked; they hadn't been beaten yet. If I fell or cried out, they would be the winners after all. I heard their cruel laughter and saw red; next thing I knew, I was kneeling on the narrow window ledge and toppling into my room. I actually saw a couple of backsides vanish into the wall.

I lay in bed for a long time, utterly exhausted by my struggles. Waves of fear and panic washed over me. A single tear formed in my right eye and rolled slowly down my cheek. It was the portent of a storm. Before I knew it, I was wracked by sobs and nearly choked in tears. It was a familiar sound in the orphanage, so no one paid it much mind. If they'd known it was Linda Lakoe putting on such a display, there'd have been a stampede up the stairwell, you can bet on that.

Slowly I got control of myself. I crept to the washroom, surveyed the damage, did my best to flood the tears out of my eyes and erase the tracks of tears from my face. I washed the brick dust off my skin and cleaned up my wounds as best I could. I couldn't do much about my frayed hem or the rip on my right sleeve. Satisfied that I'd done all I could to repair the damage, I crept back to my bedroom and lay down. For the first time in weeks I enjoyed a deep, dreamless sleep.

Hours later, I suppose, I woke up to a gentle shaking. Phyllis loomed over me, her face nearly in my own. "Linda, what's going on with you?" she whispered, urgency in her voice. "You're real late for dinner. Joseph and some others are out looking for you. C'mon."

Fittingly, Phyllis was the one who ushered me back to the land of the living, and to the dry bologna and cheese sandwich, chips, and strawberry Kool-Aid that made up our Sunday night meal. This evening the Murrow orphans ate in the hallway, on the stairs and landings, little groups of friends having fun. I sat on the steps with Jackie and Phyllis and Enid and ate my sandwich with gratitude; that night it tasted delicious.

PHOTO

15

GUARDIAN ANGEL WITH CANDELABRA

I don't know if you'll ever see him as I do, within his black and silver world. His great polished Steinway is sable black like the night sky; the flickering flames of his candelabra multiply in the mirror surfaces until they seem as multitudinous as the stars. His tuxedo sweeps down his back like wings; bat wings, I suppose, to some but angel wings to me. His sleek black hair sweeps back from his great brow; his wonderful warm smile flashes the straightest, whitest teeth imaginable. His plump fingers dance over the piano keyboard with surprising nimbleness. The music washes over me in waves as his hands run the keys in sweeping arpeggios.

Hearing Liberace play his piano was an ecstasy always, and never more so than on the evening after my brush with death. I'm not quite sure why. Maybe it was because he was all I knew of the world of art and culture, and some instinct told me that art, music, elegant clothes, lovely manners—all the things I lacked at Murrow—would prove to be my way out. Maybe it was just that Liberace was as far removed from Mrs. Joseph as a peacock from a crow.

We watched Liberace on Sunday evenings religiously. Most of us adored him, and oddly enough, Mrs. Joseph was his biggest fan. For us, Liberace was music. He was elegance, joy, light, gorgeous harmony. He was certainly the reason we gathered in the big living room on Sunday evenings.

I didn't want to sit near anyone, not even Jackie. I didn't really need to see

Liberace tonight; I knew what he looked like. One of the comforting things about him was that he always looked the same. Handsome as an angel, as I'd heard Mrs. Joseph say on more than one occasion. With a face so smooth his skin was like satin, and never a hair out of place. He always wore his wonderful tuxedo, which was as black as his piano, though it certainly didn't reflect the candles the way the piano did. He had a sweet voice too, especially when he was talking to his brother George. I liked the way he talked to George; it made me think a little differently about Jackie and family when I heard him.

But most of all I loved to hear him play the piano. This evening I just closed my eyes and listened. I could picture his hands running up and down the keyboard in time to the glorious cascades of sound. I knew they touched the keys so gently and quickly that you could hardly follow their flight. I could follow better with my eyes closed, it seemed, listening intently, imagining the dance of the responsive keys.

He played "Flight of the Bumblebee." He loved to do it, and I loved to hear it. I didn't think anyone else in the world could buzz and flutter so much like busy, swarming bees; I knew that no other human hands could move as surely as his. He played other things, I can't remember what. But I do remember that something amazing happened. Although I had never seen *Fantasia* or even heard of it, I began to see the abstract, rhythmic flashes of light and color that accompanied the first musical passage of that great and original movie. I could see the music as well as hear it. It was thrilling.

I opened my eyes for the last number of the evening. It seemed that there were even more candles than usual on the piano. I think brother George brought out an extra candlestick and they made some sort of joke about it. That didn't really matter; all that mattered was the music. And Liberace played that last number wonderfully well. His hands raced up and down the keyboard even faster than I'd imagined; sometimes he reached his left hand beyond his right, creating his trademark virtuoso effect.

When I closed my eyes again, it seemed that I could see horses running to the rhythms of his play. Now they galloped, now they cantered, now they reared in mock battle. During the most inspired passages they seemed to soar over hedges in an ecstasy of flight.

The music ended, and I opened my eyes. I saw happy faces all around; kids who'd never been friendly were nodding and smiling shyly at each other, at me. I knew then that I'd made the right choice when I pulled myself back up to the window. Heaven didn't have Liberace. Not yet.

PHOTO

16

WE TALK OF SUNDRY THINGS

Back to the horse pasture. This time not alone. Phyllis has summoned me to my own secret place. This friendship thing has drawbacks; there's no real privacy anymore, it seems. Of course, I know the pasture best. I've led the way to the old stump that's so round and big across that King Arthur could have used it for his table. We're putting it to a different use. I've brought a peach and a plum to the festivities, gifts from Mrs. Treat in honor of a new outbreak of sores. Phyllis has a belt she found on the ground outside my window. She lays the belt on the stump in a reverse S; *I place peach and plum within its two loops. Together we've made a still life, classic in its simplicity.*

I'd forgotten about the belt until Phyllis motioned me aside in school and gave me a peek inside her book bag. There it was, coiled like a snake. I worked hard to control my face and looked her in the eye. I had to know what she'd seen, what she knew. "We need to talk," she whispered. "Private. In the horse pasture after school." I'd have to wait, but not too long. Waiting was easy enough; it was something we did all the time at Murrow.

We walked to the stump in silence. I wasn't about to speak first. I wasn't giving anything away today. Actually, there were things I needed to ask Phyllis, in private. But all that would depend on what she knew about the belt and what she intended to do with what she knew. It could be that the whole friendship thing had just been a pose to get me to let down my guard. If that was true, I was in trouble. When Joseph learned about my jump, she just might have me thrown into a nut house. It was as serious as that.

Phyllis was pretty good at the uses of silence herself. She fumbled in her book bag, finally emerging with the belt. Without a word, she laid it on the stump, carefully arranging it in the shape of a backwards S. I bit my lip. Finally she broke into a smile. "Yours?" she asked.

"Yeah, I guess so," I answered, relieved by her smile. "Yeah. Where'd you find it?"

"Under your window. On the dirt right under your window. Lucky it was me found it. Somebody else might of run to Joseph, and then you'd have some questions to answer."

"You don't have any questions?" I had to ask it.

"No. I'm not askin'." God, I was lucky in her. "If you needed to give your little sister a whipping, believe me, I can understand that. But wrap it around your hand, that way it won't go flying out the window." She winked at me. I don't know to this day whether she actually saw me out on the ledge or hanging by a hook from the building. If she did, then my hat's off to her. I couldn't have stopped myself asking if the tables had been turned.

"Yeah, that's the way it was," I lied. "Sometimes she about drives me crazy. But, uh, hasn't anyone missed this yet?"

"Laundry's not for a couple of days," she reminded me. "That's when she'll check all the clothes." She tapped the belt buckle. "I'm gonna leave it to you to put this back where it oughta be."

"Okay, thanks." I thought about my peach and plum and fished them out of my pocket. "Take the one you want," I offered. She took the peach and put it in the belt loop nearest her. I did the same with my plum. I couldn't help noticing the pattern that was forming on the stump and pointing it out. "Lookit. Kinda pretty, yes?"

Phyllis looked. She laughed a happy laugh. "You're so good at art," she complimented. "I wish I was." There, she'd brought up the very subject I wanted to ask her about.

"Funny you say that," I replied. "I don't know about how good I am or anything, but I did want to ask you something . . . I guess it's about art. You see, there's something I want to draw . . . I'm planing to draw . . . for that art contest, you know. But I don't really know . . . well, I guess I just don't know what it looks like."

"I never been to a zoo, neither, if that's what you're askin' about." She sounded kind of angry.

"No, nothin' like that," I hastened to say. "It's . . . you were telling us about the thing your people, your grandma, I think it was, believe in. You know, the big, real big tree over that canyon, with our world on one side, where the roots are, and the other world over by the branches. I can't get that out of my mind. But I don't know . . . I don't know enough about how it looks. Not to draw it. So I need you."

You could tell this was about the last thing Phyllis expected me to bring up. But I could see she was thinking about what to say. "She never drew it for me or nothin'," she said at last, "so I don't know how much help I can be. Maybe if you ask some questions . . ."

"I need to know how big if I'm gonna put people on it, which I am. I mean, is it like one of the big trees hereabouts? Or is it lots bigger yet?"

Phyllis looked thoughtful. "I don't know. Not even grandma. Nobody knows these things; nobody I ever heard of really seen that tree. But I've thought about it, and I figure it's got to be a whole lot bigger than any other tree. You can't see across to the other side, and you can see a pretty long way. But I don't think it's the same for everybody. It's not a real tree, like these others."

"Whattaya mean?" I couldn't tell her that I'd seen it, or something a whole lot like it, myself.

"I mean you couldn't burn it or make a chair out of it. You couldn't even see it if you wasn't about to cross over yourself. So what I think is that it's just as big as it needs to be. For some people the good place is way far off. For others it's probably so close they don't even need a tree; they could just step over."

I had to think about that for a while. It wasn't what I expected, but it did make sense. If you were good, if you hadn't done any person or creature harm, you just stepped over. Or maybe you walked a ways, but it was like walking on a black-topped highway, even with a red carpet rolled out for you. But if you'd been real bad and done harm to people or critters, then that tree would be long and skinny, like one of those ropes the circus people walk on. The wind would be howling, and all those enemies you made would be tugging at your legs and shaking the tree, and you'd be inching your way along. Yeah, that made a lot of sense.

"So I could make the tree just as big as I wanted it to be?"

"Don't see why not."

"And over on the other side, what do you think? I mean, you know, if you were gonna draw it?"

"I know how it would be for me," she started to speak quickly, like she'd thought about this, like she'd wished about it so hard that it was burned in her memory and her heart. "It would be green, like it is here maybe two weeks in May. Green all the time; I hate this parched-out brown. Lots of rivers, clean, clear-water rivers with fish jumping. Groves of trees like pecans and peaches and nobody watching over them, so you could just eat when you wanted. Those drive-in restaurants all over, and movie theaters, and stores with pretty dresses. And hardly any grown-ups, just enough to, you know, run the restaurants and stores and things."

"Nobody to tell you what to do?" I couldn't help jumping into her fantasy.

"Nobody with rules at all!" She was clear on that point. "If anything, the grown-ups would do what we told them. Girls our age would do whatever running things needed to be done."

"What about boys?" This was getting real good.

"Boys? I don't know what they were put on earth for, anyhow. No boys."

Now I had the idea. "Maybe on leashes. How about a few boys, but on leashes. To carry heavy stuff."

"Well, maybe." We were both running with this now. "But they would have to be real strong leashes. Boys could just mess the whole thing up without really trying."

Fish for the catching and orchards ripe for the picking, girls like Phyllis and me in charge, grown-ups running the stores and restaurants and taking our orders, boys on leashes—it all sounded wonderful. And my paradise would have other good things, personal things. All the porcelain horses you could want, for one thing. And real ones too, but very tame. Liberace playing the piano, playing my favorite songs whenever I wanted. A mom and dad for Jackie, if that wouldn't get in the way of my freedom.

It all sounded so good, as I thought it over, that I wondered whether I shouldn't have jumped after all. But then I thought about how little that tree looked and how enemies like Rachel and maybe even Jackie would be tugging at my legs and trying to shake the trunk. Maybe I'd be one who wouldn't make it across, who would plunge into the abyss.

"Y'know, I was thinkin'." I hated to splash cold water on all this lovely speculating, but I had to ask. "What if we wasn't the ones to make it across? I got enemies, you know. Rachel and . . . well . . . lots of others."

"Rachel." Phyllis spit when she said it. "Don't you just hate her? Big, ugly bully. I bet she'd be about as big as an old daddy-long-legs trying to tip over that log. All your enemies are there, sure, but they ain't all life-size. I wouldn't worry about Rachel."

I never knew Phyllis felt the same way about Rachel as I did. God, I'd love to get even with that girl. Now, with an ally, maybe I could do it. "Ever think about getting back at Rachel?" I tried to keep all the longing out of my voice and make it just a simple question.

"Get back? Well, she don't beat me up like she does you. Not that she'd dare." Phyllis said that with an assurance that I could never match. It reminded me that she was a queen at Murrow, something I could never hope to be. "But her nasty ways just spoil things at the orphanage. Yeah, I could get back at her for making so many little girls cry. I could just do that thing." She paused and looked at me. "You know," she said with real admiration in her eyes, "if you didn't fight Rachel, she'd run that place. If you didn't fight her, it'd be up to me. I'd have to."

We both considered that prospect for a minute. I had never thought of Phyllis as a fighter, but she had taken on the bullies at school that day I was locked in the infirmary. Maybe she had it in her. But I couldn't imagine Rachel losing much sleep over the prospect.

"I'm not talking about fighting her," I said. "Not even about beating her up. I'm talking about gettin' even. I mean, humiliating her. In front of everybody."

"I know what you mean." Phyllis sounded very sure about that. "It's only that beatin' would be easier. This other, that'll take a lot of thinking. We'll have to work out all the details just so."

And that's just what we did for maybe a quarter of an hour: sat silent and thought of humiliations for Rachel. It was only too easy to imagine her all wet or filthy or puking her guts out right there in the yard, in front of everybody. It was so easy that it did no good at all. Because the question of how to do it wasn't answered by picturing Rachel in varied permutations of distress.

"I wish Ruthie was here," Phyllis said. "Nobody was ever better'n her at coming up with great schemes. That girl's a clever one."

Ruthie. If only Ruthie were here, indeed. I realized all at once, once again, how very much I missed her. I'd heard nothing but woeful tidings about Ruthie since the night she ran off with Elmer. Could it be that Phyllis knew something definite, something more hopeful than the swirl of rumor and speculation that surrounded the vanished Ruthie?

"I don't know," I answered. "From what I've heard, Ruthie needs all that cleverness and more just to help herself."

"Oh, what have you heard, then?" Phyllis demanded.

"Well, that she's left Elmer, for one thing. That she's starving and stealing food. That she's written letters begging for money. Even that she and Elmer are in jail. All sorts of bad things."

"Oh, it's probably Rachel and her kind spreading that stuff." Phyllis shook her head contemptuously. "I'm surprised you even listened to that. Ruthie's living somewhere in Tulsa, from what we hear. Working in a Kresge's and going to school at night. Living with one of my aunts."

"One of your aunts?" I was amazed.

"Well, yeah. She's like a cousin . . . a distant cousin. Didn't you know that?" A shake of my head was my only answer. "It's true. And now that she can pay her way, one of my aunts is giving her a place to stay."

I looked at Phyllis with a new regard. Ruthie's cousin, indeed. It seemed that all sorts of good things flowed through Phyllis.

"Hey, listen," I said, my heart in my mouth, "you think you can actually get something to Ruthie?"

She thought about it for a minute. "Well, maybe not right away," she replied. "But I don't see why . . . sure, I'm pretty sure we could."

I turned away and removed one of my porcelain ponies from its secret hiding place. "When she left, she gave me a little horse. But I didn't know, so I didn't have a chance to give her nothing. I'd sure like her to have one of these. If you could do that . . ."

Phyllis picked it up, gave it a good look, and put it down on the stump next to her peach. Then, without a word, she took out one of her grandmother's beaded combs and put it next to my plum. She picked up the peach and the porcelain; I hid away my belt and comb and began to eat my plum. We walked out of the horse pasture together, in silence, each bearing treasured gifts.

I've never been sure whether Phyllis was able to give that porcelain pony to Ruthie. Maybe she just kept it for herself. It doesn't really matter. Either way is just fine with me because either way that little porcelain is with a true friend.

PHOTO
17

THE HOUNDS OF BACONE

It is right out the window, by the teetertotters and slicker slides. They've told us to stay away from the window, but how can we not look? Our big boys, who work the farm, are gathered with bows and arrows. They're expert shots. Some of the men from the farm—white men in overalls with dark beards and stern, glowering expressions—are there too. Indians from Bacone in business suits take their place in the circle. The men don't seem as comfortable with their weapons, don't hold the bows like they want to use them. But they are grim in their determination. Sitting and prowling and growling among the playground equipment is a pack of wild dogs. A couple of them are giants, snapping and snarling; most are smallish country mutts, coats snarled and ribs showing. I recognize the mother and pup who began to visit us a couple of weeks ago. One of the big dogs approaches the men, threatening. An arrow flies; I see him fall. "Girls, please, this isn't for you to see." There is real worry in Mrs. Joseph's voice. "This is something we have to do. We can't have any of our precious babies hurt." She sweeps me and two of the girls near me up into her arms. We tremble; so does she. The high-pitched yelps and whines of dying dogs fill the air. Mrs. Joseph ushers us all into the kitchen and keeps us there until a truck arrives and hauls away the dog corpses. The dust around the slides is stained dark red; nobody plays on them until after the next rain.

When the brown-and-white terrier and her plump little pup first wandered into our Murrow grounds, we were tickled. We could not have imagined where the innocent intrusion would lead. Jackie and I were wary at first; most of the dogs we'd known at our foster homes had been surly and half-wild. You were well advised to keep out of their way. Phyllis must have had some bad experience with dogs; looking into her face as she shrank back from the pair, I saw fear. But timid little Eunice Cloud went right up to the mother, moving very calmly and slowly and talking in a voice that was as soothing as wind blowing through the grass.

"Pretty girl," she said. "Such a pretty pup. Nobody's gonna hurt you or your sweet baby." The scared, wild mama curled her thin lips and showed fangs. She hunkered down on her haunches and her eyes widened, staring her fear. She was ready to tear the arm or throat of anyone who threatened her pup. I backed off; most everyone else did too. But Eunice reached out her arm, so slowly you could hardly see it move, and crooned her reassuring message. "Nobody's gonna hurt you girl; nobody's gonna do you no harm." Eunice's gentle little fingers stretched out toward the black nose. The fingers touched; the dog trembled and shook, started back, and stopped. In a minute Eunice was scratching her behind the ears; before sunset the scared, wild dog was rolling on her back, feet in the air, while Eunice scratched her tummy.

Simon Whiteturkey and Ralph Timm knew more than a little about dogs themselves. Simon went to fetch some kitchen scraps, which the mother gobbled greedily. Ralph fetched a little dish of milk for the pup, and before even the mother knew it, he'd scooped up the little fellow and was stroking him in his lap.

Eunice, Simon, and Ralph remained in charge of the dogs they'd tamed. Responsibility for supplying food, milk, and water fell to them. The rest of us made our tentative approaches and reached our own uneasy truces with the pair. I think we all started to feel like the dogs had become pets of the orphanage, and what was particularly sweet about it was that the adults seemed to have nothing to say in the matter. We'd done the taming, after all; we'd earned the right to keep these animals. Certainly they were doing nobody any harm.

Then the big stray came to haunt Big Planet. He appeared to be a shepherd, only longer and lankier. Simon took one look at him and proclaimed, "That one's got wolf blood in him, I'll swear it. Lookit the way he lopes over that big ole Planet. Just eats up the ground, without even running. I heard of wolves doin' that. Not dogs though, just wolves."

The wolf never came near us. And needless to say, Big Planet became off-limits for our play. I didn't like it; it wasn't a good trade-off as far as I was concerned. I liked the freedom of Big Planet better than I liked being tenth in line for the affections of a stray dog. But there were times, when I got to play with that puppy, that it almost seemed like a fair deal. The pup was that cute.

There was a connection between the wolf and the terrier. She'd go out to him, then return to us. She couldn't call him in; he couldn't compel her to stay out. There was tension between them, growing and soon to break. Either he'd come in to us at last, tail wagging, a convert to domestication, or he'd come with fangs bared, ready to kill. The terrier showed signs of his influence when she came in from Big Planet: she'd snap and growl, and it took all of Eunice's patience and love to soothe her wild nature and make her our pet again. Still, the tension grew, and all us orphans felt it. Why wouldn't that half-wolf just go and leave us in peace? We didn't want to lose our new pets, but we didn't want to live in fear either.

It seemed that we kids were the only ones aware of the drama. Finally, Phyllis, the one of us who was most afraid of the great shaggy hound of Bacone, pointed him out to Mrs. Joseph. "Yes ma'am, he's been out there a week," she said, exaggerating just a bit. "I hardly dare play outside anymore." Mrs. Joseph didn't seem to react, but time would prove that she'd taken the words to heart.

Then the drama took an unexpected turn. The standoff between wolf and terrier continued, but gradually, day by day, the wild dog was joined by new members of what soon became a pack. Now, strays were by no means out of the ordinary in rural Oklahoma; people were always dropping off unwanted pets in the country. But a pack of a dozen or more wild dogs posed a real threat to everyone—kids, grown-ups, even livestock on the nearby farm. We traveled in groups, and Joseph hovered over us like a shepherd guarding her sheep. We kept a wary eye on the dogs in Big Planet, and they kept a close watch on us. Twice Mrs. Joseph summoned the men with bows and guns, but the cautious dogs scattered into the brush. Some of the timid girls had trouble eating and took to crying in their sleep.

"You must not feed the puppy anymore, none of you," Joseph ordered, and most of us agreed. But mother and baby wouldn't leave us now; they seemed nearly as frightened of the gathering pack as we. And Eunice couldn't bear to see her little pup hungry. I never quite managed to follow her, but I know that she snuck food out to her special pets.

The boys organized a watch. Like prairie dogs, we kept our eyes open as we worked and played. And one day, as the heat bounced in shimmering lines from the dry grass of the prairie, Simon cried out, "They're coming; the dogs is coming." We saw them run toward our Murrow grounds, their legs wavering like smoke in the heat. They didn't make a sound as they ran. We scrambled indoors and watched from windows as the dog pack occupied our playground. The terrier and her pup were among them; they hadn't been quick enough to follow our lead.

Mrs. Joseph hurried to the phone and made one, two, three calls. The white farmworkers arrived first, then the Indian boys, and finally the men from Bacone. They were armed with bows and arrows so there would be less chance of shooting each other in the melee.

I couldn't keep away from the window, though I didn't want to witness the slaughter. I saw the first arrow fired, heard the first death scream, watched a smallish mutt I didn't know writhe in its agony. Mrs. Joseph hugged me to her and pulled me away, pulled all of us away, down to the kitchen where we couldn't see. She gave us a treat of animal crackers and milk—a special treat, really—but we could hear the whining and yelping just outside, so none of us ate very much. It seemed like it went on a long time, longer than a day, though I know that couldn't have been so. We stayed in a while after the shouts and cries stopped, until a noisy truck drove in and then drove out again.

Mrs. Joseph seemed as afraid, as appalled, as relieved as the rest of us, while we waited for the horror to end. "I've been so afraid for all of you," she said, her voice quavering. "Dogs can be wonderful," she said, looking straight at Eunice as she spoke, "but they can also be terribly dangerous . . . the wild ones. I've been so afraid this last week; I didn't want to let you know how scared I was. Oh, girls, it's going to be all right." I felt good knowing she cared that much. I hugged Jackie and Phyllis; we all hugged each other as the horrible noise peaked and faded. Only Eunice was outside our circle.

Mrs. Joseph never mentioned the dread word *rabies;* none of us did. But it was on our minds. It was the ultimate threat the dogs posed, the true reason they had to be killed. Wild dogs who moved into a peopled place had to be suspect, had to be feared.

When it was all over and the bodies had been carted away, we ventured back out to our playground. The dirt had been dug up by claws and turned over by spades. The men had tried to wash out the dark bloodstains, but some had withstood their best efforts. The terrier and her pup had vanished with the rest. Mrs. Joseph told us that one of the farmers had taken them, but I don't think I believed it. I know Eunice didn't. I didn't return to play on the slicker slide until a rain had washed the remnants of blood from the soil. Eunice never did go back. But I think even she knew that the thing they'd done was something that had had to be done.

PHOTO
18

I MEET THE MASTER

A big cork bulletin board. The kind that opens out into an **A** *to stand freely in a school corridor. It is hung with typical children's drawings. I remember a clown, very well drawn, with enormous feet, a balloon man holding a giant bunch of rainbow-colored balloons and floating over the heads of children, and an apple tree on a hill. They were done by white students from Muskogee schools and had gold, red, and blue ribbons hung next to them, first, second, and third prize in our annual art contest. My picture is also displayed on the board—on the front, just below the prize winners. It is the most prominent position ever occupied by an Indian drawing, and I'm proud of it. We student-artists are assembled in a small group off to the side. I've hidden myself next to the wall, but I stand on tiptoe to see what the gathered dignitaries are looking at, and it seems to me that many are returning for a closer look at my painting. One in particular, a handsome Indian man in a dark suit, spends what seems quite a long time studying my work. His concentration is so intense that he doesn't seem to notice the ring of open space and respectful silence that forms around him.*

I'd done it. I'd gotten the attention of Rogers School at last, and I hadn't had to march publicly into the white-only bathroom to do it. So much better, I'd made my way onto the white-only bulletin board that showed off the best art produced by grammar-school students, not only at Rogers but in all of Muskogee. I hadn't won any of their stupid ribbons, but it was plain to see that the lion's share of attention was coming my way.

And no wonder. My drawing may not have been as good, technically speaking, as the excellent clown drawn by a boy from a school across town. After all, his subject was a clown, and mine was a whole world, packed with detail and alive with wonder. I'd been able to draw the great tree Phyllis and I had talked about in the horse pasture and the other world, the perfect world beyond, just as I imagined it should be. I had taped two big pieces of construction paper together to do it.

On the left sheet I had drawn the tree. It had real big roots, and people of all ages were climbing up those roots to get on the trunk. Other people—loved ones and family—were waving and blowing kisses to help their friends make the crossing. A steep cliff plunged down into a chasm obscured by thick, billowing smoke; flames and lightnings flashed in the clouds down there. The trunk itself was thick and gnarly and colored like the rainbow; green, yellow, red, and violet branches grew up from it. Old people and grown-ups and kids were all crossing the trunk. Some were beset by big, powerful enemies; some walked easily; some were carried in their mothers' arms; some fell off into the abyss. The ones who made it across climbed through a great tangle of luxurious branches into the righthand sheet, where I'd drawn my personal paradise.

There were horses running free all over the plain, and because this was my fantasy, I was riding a whole bunch of them at the same time. Liberace was playing his piano right out in the open, under the spreading green branches. Candlesticks were set up in a giant circle around his piano, and I was the only one sitting within that circle. There were dress stores and doll stores. Right out under the blue sky I had a giant dollhouse with all the cutest little curlyheaded blond dolls you can imagine just waiting to play with me. Mrs. Treat had a big, modern kitchen on the grounds. She had cast-iron kettles and pans on the stove, with all my favorite foods boiling and bubbling merrily within. I'd drawn the other girls facing temporary walls erected just for that purpose, while I sat with a few of my friends at a table heaped high with good things to eat. This was my paradise, after all. Boys on leashes? You bet there were. One of my incarnations held a sturdy leash in each hand, boys in choke collars submissively awaiting my command.

I really didn't know much about tipis—I'd certainly never seen one—but I set up a circle of tipis at the upper right corner of my paradise. I knew they were Indian for one thing, and I couldn't think of any place to live that looked less like the dark brick and stone of the Murrow Orphanage.

So there it was: the Kiowa tree leading to a paradise that was strictly the property of Linda Lakoe. I planned and sketched out every feature before applying it to paper with watercolor, cut and pasted paper, or crayola. The effect of the whole was of a fabulous intricacy of color, texture, subject, and action that enthralled me. I kept adding things, stepping back, and raising my fist in triumph. Everything I did seemed to work. I titled it "Kiowa Tree between This World and the Next." I don't think anything I've ever painted has given me greater pleasure. I never imagined that I had the power to create such a thing until I actually sat down and made my Kiowa tree.

The distinguished Indian gentleman in the dark suit spent some minutes in discussion with my principal, who then came over to personally escort me to meet the great man. "Mr. West, this is Linda Lakoe," was all she said.

With a grave but kind expression on his face and the barest hint of a smile playing about his lips, the man extended his hand. I was plenty scared, but I couldn't help noticing what a remarkable hand it was. The fingers were long and supple, the skin weathered, the fingertips tinted with pigments that just wouldn't wash out. The hands suggested precision and control; they reminded me of the power and precision of Liberace's hands on a piano keyboard.

"Young lady, where did this come from?" he asked in a rich baritone.

I didn't know what he was asking. I looked down at my feet and answered the best I could. "I made it all," I muttered. "I made everything on that paper all by myself."

"I'm sure you did," he reassured me. "That wasn't my meaning."

There was nothing more for me to say, so I stood silent.

"What I'm wondering," he tried to explain, "is how do you know about the Kiowa tree? You're not Kiowa, are you?"

97

"I'm Apache." I needed to be careful. Maybe Phyllis had told me more than she should have. Maybe I'd painted something that was out of bounds for me. "But I don't know about Apache. My friend told me about this. I took a liking to it right away. Did we do somethin' wrong?"

He took my hands in his and looked deep into my eyes. He had dark, knowing, sad eyes. "You did just fine, honey. Better than fine. Now, who's this friend of yours? Maybe I know her."

"Phyllis Marie Goodbear," I answered, as formally as I could. "She's Kiowa."

"Ah, Phyllis," he said, as if that explained something.

"You know Phyllis?"

"I think about everybody at Bacone knows Phyllis," he answered. Which must have been the biggest exaggeration I'd heard in a long time. It put me on my guard; I didn't want to get Phyllis in trouble.

"It's not her fault, none of it," I said as firmly as I could. "Phyllis didn't tell me none of these details. Well, mostly not. She said the good place, after you pass over, she thought that place was probably a little different for everybody. Depending on the things you like. So I just put a lot of the things I like over there, is all. Take Liberace playing his piano. I really like him, is why he's there."

Mr. West smiled and shook his head. Apparently I'd just cleared up a little mystery for him. He reached out his hand again and shook mine. "Young lady," he said, "please, don't let anyone ever tell you that you shouldn't be painting the Kiowa tree. It's exactly the sort of thing you should be painting. It's the sort of thing I should be painting myself. Miss Linda Lakoe, my name is Richard West. It's been a great pleasure to meet you."

It wasn't for a couple of hours that I recognized the name Richard West. Then it occurred to me: that was the name written in paint on the bottom righthand corner of the great altar mural at the Bacone College chapel. And that was the most beautiful thing I'd ever seen in the whole world. Wow!

PHOTO
19

WHEN ONLY AN APACHE WILL DO

Not all circles are the same. I'm something of an expert on circles; for someone who most certainly is a loner, I find myself at their center more often than I can understand or explain. This circle is different from the others I've found myself in. Its circumference is composed mostly of boys. They are not in close contact; indeed, they've spread out as far as their sense of honor will allow. Morbid curiosity is the gravity that holds us together; real fear is the centrifugal force that throws us apart. A sort of solar system is the result. Simon leads me to the center of the thin, uneven circle of boys, and girls too, to the burlap bag that is thrashing and caterwauling in the dust. Nothing makes such cries except a cat in pain. They've told me the story; I know what I must do. Blood has seeped through the bag, staining it a dark brown; there are smears of brown blood on the ground. Even so, I feel I must look into the bag to confirm the story I've been told. The cat is horrifying: its fur is soaked in drying blood; its toothless, bleeding gum is broken and hanging; one eye socket is empty. I shudder and bite my lip. Simon helps me retie the bag. "Forgive me," I whisper to the cat. It answers with a low moan that raises the hair on the back of my neck. I find its head and bring a rock down as hard as I can; I know I won't be able to strike again. The bag jerks for a few minutes, then stops. I rise up from the dust and walk silently through the scattered boys and girls. No one walks with me.

The day I put the cat out of its misery dawned like any other. It was a routine day at school. The brief flurry of excitement surrounding the art contest had died down, and we were once again securely in the grip of monotony. While I was going through the motions at school, one of our orphanage cats was embarking on its last adventure. Yes, we did have cats; they patrolled the kitchens and dorm basements, keeping the population of mice under control. Cats roamed the college grounds and farm outbuildings, nesting in the straw on cold nights. But they weren't pets, though some of us tried to tame them with bits of food stolen from the dinner table and even plates of milk accumulated a drop at a time from many glasses. Furtive and wild, they would slip from the shadows to snatch a bit of meat or lap at a dish of milk, but any advance on our part would send them scurrying away. Sometimes, when they thought they were alone, they would bask in the sun out on the Big Planet, but we could never approach soundlessly enough to surprise them in their sun-drenched stupor. Invariably they ran off hissing if we succeeded in getting close.

It's a measure of our need that so many little orphans continued the one-sided wooing. I'd given it up long ago; I figured the cats were a little like me—when they wanted to be alone, that was that. So I let them pretty much alone. But Jackie was Jackie. She was single-minded in her pursuit of the family of orange tabbies, which were by far the cutest of the lot. She would track them with all the concentration and patience she could muster; once she was rewarded for a specially good effort with a nasty scratch running the length of her left arm.

Jackie begged me to help, and since I was the main obstacle in her pursuit of parents, I felt I owed her my best effort to procure a pet. Sometimes, armed with tidbits of food and the ability to move without a sound, I did get within petting range of one of the half-grown orange tabbies that were not yet confirmed in their wildness. Then I would gently and cautiously rub its head or scratch it behind the ears; once a tabby even relaxed into the humming vibration of its purr. But invariably Jackie would rush in, squealing with delight, and the nervous, half-wild kitty would reward me with a hiss and a scratch.

At the conclusion of one such drama, Jackie said, not meaning it as a compliment to either of us, "Linda, those cats are so much like you—impossible to love." Somehow she had put my own sentiment into words, and I resolved not to bother the cats anymore, especially not on her account.

I honored that resolve until the day in question. It was a day in early autumn, but unseasonably hot. The air was heavy. The birds had evidently sought out the shade of trees and barn eaves. The chorus of birdsong that usually filled the brisk air of fall was absent. As I stepped off the school bus I was aware of the silence of birds and children and of a barely audible shriek beneath the silence, as if the dry grass and trees were crying out in a voice beyond human hearing. I saw a scattering of children gathered in dumb anguish on a distant corner of the grounds; I'd never seen the boys so subdued, abashed, and helpless looking. Phyllis and I exchanged shrugs; instinctively, I pulled Jackie close. Something was wrong, but not one of the usual somethings.

Simon came up to me with some of his friends. Actually, it seemed that he was reluctant, that they were pulling him to me, pulling against his own powerful sense of shame. He was the only boy who knew me well enough to ask the favor they needed of me.

"Linda," he said, and then fell silent.

"Simon?"

"There's something . . . has to be done. And, um, well, nobody can do it." His shame was in his voice; the other two boys actually looked away.

"There's a lot of boys here," I couldn't help observing.

"Maybe it takes an Apache, is what we're thinking." The boys who were with him nodded in silent agreement.

"Well, I don't know. You best tell me, then." I didn't know what he was talking about, but I knew I wasn't going to want to do it.

"It's one of the cats. C'mon, I better show you." Simon took me by the hand. He walked slowly, reluctantly. By now I could see the burlap sack squirming on the ground; I could hear the moans, which sounded like a police siren when they rose to a high-pitched wail.

"One of the tabbies," Simon explained. "Car hit it, must have been. God, Linda, it's in such terrible shape. It's gonna die for sure. But it's suffering so bad. We gotta put it out of its misery."

We? What did he mean by "we"? All those boys, most of them bigger than me, and they wanted me to do the deed? "Take a rock and do it then, one of you guys. You, Simon. I mean if it needs to be done. I don't know why you're waiting around for me. Why me?"

"I couldn't do it." He looked sheepish when he said it. "None of us. We all heard, you know, about how Apaches could do . . . well, things that needed to be done. Hard things, tough things. Scalping . . . well we all, and whites too. But, you know, things that scared the whole frontier. Anyway, I'm not saying anything bad. Just that for some things maybe you need an Apache."

All of them, all the big boys in that circle, looked at me as if they agreed with Simon. And, believe me, I'd heard it before, variations of it. Apaches were a breed apart. Ferocity, fight, endurance, the ability to suffer heat, cold, pain—these were the traits that defined us. So it was only natural that Simon and the rest would think of me when they needed someone to bash in the cat's skull. And only natural that I would agree; I was Apache, as we all understood the word.

Simon warned me against opening the bag. "You don't want to do that. Please don't." But I couldn't take the chance that they were setting me up or that they'd exaggerated the extent of injury in their panic. I also wanted to see if it might be a cat I knew; I wanted to say goodbye.

One glimpse told me all I needed to know. I'd never be certain that it was the same cat that had once purred beneath my fingers. The best thing was to act as if it were. "Forgive me," I whispered to it as it thrashed and moaned and bled in its sack. "There's only one way I can help you now, and I'm gonna. Peace to you." I don't think anyone heard me, even though the silence was absolute, like the quiet of a cave. Simon handed me a rock. I didn't look around, didn't see anyone. I wanted this to be quick, like an eyeblink. I found the head in the squirming bag and brought the rock down with every ounce of strength I possessed. The crack of rock on bone sounded like a shot in the silence. The bag twitched for a minute, then stilled. I rose up from the dust; no one helped me or talked to me or reached out a hand to me. I walked through the ragged circle that parted for me, as stern and silent as Gary Cooper at the end of *High Noon*. I didn't eat dinner that night; no one seemed surprised.

A strange thing happened after I killed the cat. I overheard people talking about it. From what Jackie and Phyllis told me, it was quite the topic of conversation around Murrow for days. But no one ever said a word about it directly to me. They did comment in other ways. When Jackie and I got on or off the bus, the other kids kind of stepped back, making an aisle. The big girls stopped hassling Jackie; even the white kids at school seemed to know what had happened. In any case, they didn't badger and provoke as they had before. A couple of them even made an effort to talk to us and to include us in some of their playground games at recess.

I didn't realize what was happening for a while; I wasn't especially sensitive to other people, I guess. But after a week or so, Jackie pointed it out to me. "Notice anything strange goin' on?" she asked. I had to admit that I didn't. "I mean, people treatin' you different, us different. Not pickin' fights, anything like that."

Now that she mentioned it, I realized that I hadn't been in any sort of fight in more than a week. That was probably some kind of record for me. "I think it has to do with the day you killed the cat," Jackie went on. "It's like they respect us more, or somethin'. Respect you, but me too. As Apaches."

"Well, we've always been Apaches," I said.

"Yeah, sure." She was getting a little impatient. "But I think they're just now figuring out what that means."

As if to prove her right, someone slipped an extra apple onto my tray at lunch that day. Jackie got an extra banana. The world sure could be a puzzling place. And some of the surprises turned out to be good ones.

PHOTO
20

IT'S BLOWING IN THE WIND

At Murrow change, which always came about with glacial slowness, could start with a hole in the ground. The door of a black stretch limousine opens to release a tall man in a shiny blue polyester suit. It seems that we've been standing in line waiting for him for hours. We're all wearing those white-blouse, brown-skirt uniforms that are reserved for state occasions. We're lined up by height so we'll make a pretty picture. The sun sets earlier these days; our shadows stretch out far beyond our height before the distinguished guest arrives. Mrs. Treat's dinner is getting cold in the kitchen, waiting for the end of the ceremony. The sight of a long, low limousine driving up our dirt road, kicking up a cloud of dust, is so remarkable that it seems almost to justify the wait. The official emerges, shakes hands with a wavering line of old dignitaries who have some connection with the orphanage, says a very few words about a "groundbreaking program" to put orphan children together with some sort of parents, wields a new steel shovel to dig three very shallow holes, and then poses for pictures with uniformed Indian orphans. Back in the limo, and the cloud of dust is retreating down our road in just about the time it takes to read this.

It wasn't all that unusual for us to be visited by minor dignitaries. Forty years ago, long before it was a point of pride or a public-relations slogan, Oklahoma was Indian Country, and the care of the large population of Indian orphans was something of a sticking point with whatever administration happened to be in power. Thanks primarily to Mrs. Alice B. Joseph, Murrow was a model of efficiency. But the arid isolation and reliance on discipline and child labor had caught the attention of a progressive contingent. I'd heard nothing of Dr. Spock and his new gospel of child rearing, but I now suspect that the good doctor's hands were on the ceremonial shovel that dug those three portentous holes in our damp, heavy dirt.

The holes announced a grand experiment at Murrow. We were to explore the novel idea of families for orphans. The way Mrs. Joseph explained it was that they'd build three stone cabins and move a couple into each one. Then they'd rotate groups of kids through the houses, giving us our own beds, drawers, dishes, towels, and clothes to go along with our own temporary moms and dads. It was a can't-miss, something-for-everyone kind of offer. Most of the little ones, like Jackie, would have jumped at the mom-and-dad side of the package even if that'd meant living in caves dug into a hillside. I was taken with the idea of having clothes that nobody else would wear and a desk with drawers for my own paper and crayons and all. Phyllis was very excited by the promise of a kitchen where she might have a chance to practice what apparently were already formidable cooking skills. Truly something for everyone.

After the holes were dug, it became clear that the painfully slow pace of the groundbreaking would set the tone for the entire project. In the time it took to move in the steam shovels and dump trucks we kids could have dug out the foundations with little beach shovels and pails, I swear we could. Indeed, some of us took to hanging around the building site and aiding the professionals by sneaking into the excavation to help dig it out.

Phyllis and I gave up our play in Big Planet so we could speed up the slow tease of the construction. She was enthusiastic about the project and quite certain that she would be one of the very first to occupy a cottage. While we worked, she would talk about all the good times she expected to have in the stone mansion she envisioned rising above our heads. She had wonderful plans for meals and parties. I don't know where she came by her knowledge of cooking; she would only offer the suggestion that her grandmother had been renowned in the tribe for her skill in the kitchen. Although I was an ardent believer in Mrs. Treat's culinary mastery, I had to admit that nothing we ever had at Murrow came anywhere near the wondrous dinners Phyllis described as we dug away baskets of the heavy Oklahoma clay. She talked about birds and small game—duck and quail and prairie chicken, rabbit stew, possum, squirrel pie, venison—things I'd never eaten but had heard other kids, children of Indian country, talk about. She knew about catfish and grits and cornbread and hominy and fried chicken and country fried steak, the staples of Oklahoma cooking that did sometimes pass through Mrs. Treat's kitchen and make their way to our dinner plates. Boy, I'll tell you, when Phyllis got to talking about the meals she'd cook in her very own kitchen, I got to thinking, forget about that couple, I want to be one of Phyllis's kids, living in her cabin and eating from her wonderful menu.

I was willing to believe that Phyllis would be one of the first to move into the new group homes; it seemed that she was one of the select few at Murrow who sometimes got what they wanted. I didn't begrudge her that; I thought she pretty well deserved it. On the other hand, I figured that Jackie and I would be at the absolute bottom of the list. After every single other kid at Murrow had passed through the cottages, and moss had grown into the cracks in the limestone, a twenty-five-year-old Jackie and I might possibly get a chance to bask in the attention of pseudoparents. Little Apaches seemed to be at the very bottom of the list of desirable daughters.

And then something completely unforeseen happened. Mrs. Lynette Reeve, from the tiny hamlet of Winganon, Oklahoma, came to our orphanage looking for an Indian baby to adopt and met the Lakoe girls. I assumed for many weeks that she'd seen Jackie at play, made inquiries, learned that we were joined at the hip, and decided, in view of the paucity of babies on hand, to justify her drive by talking to us. I learned that the true story was a little different. She'd actually asked Mrs. Joseph whether any of the older orphans had special talents. The memory of my notable triumph in the recent Muskogee school art contest being fresh in her mind, the good woman saw fit to describe me as one of the very best young artists in the state. That will give you some idea of the lengths she was willing to go to to get us adopted.

There wasn't time for us to get dressed up or anything. Mrs. Joseph just called us in and presented us to this strange woman. She sat at the table, so it wasn't easy to tell how tall she was. She wore a pink sweater with little pearl buttons; it looked like she had a gray skirt on under the table. She wasn't dressed all frilly and perky like most of the women who came to check out the pickings at Murrow; she was dressed sensibly, I guess. She wasn't young, certainly, but she wasn't old, and she hadn't let herself go to fat. She had a strong, attractive face. Though she certainly looked white, there was something about her cheekbones, her high forehead, and the cast of her eyes that didn't look out of place at Bacone. Her hands seemed strong, with long fingers; she was twisting a scarf that had been on her head back and forth in her hands, so I guess she was nervous.

"Hello, girls," she said and then didn't seem to know what else to say. Jackie wasn't doing much talking; she liked the fat women in flower-print dresses who paraded before us from time to time. I kind of liked this Mrs. Reeve, whose clothes, at least, said no nonsense. But I wasn't the one who would keep the conversation alive. "Mrs. Joseph told me a little about you," she finally said. "So I have an advantage on you. Let me tell you a little about me." She smiled when she said it, and I was surprised to find that I really was interested. She had a wonderful smile, warm and sincere, nothing phony about it.

"My husband and I live on a nice little farm about seventy-five miles north and east of here," she continued. "We have cattle, about forty head, chickens for eggs, some ducks and geese." I knew just the kind of place she was talking about; Jackie and I had been foster slaves at little farms just like it. They lived in "a white frame house with two bedrooms, a comfortable living room. The toilet, unfortunately, is outdoors, but you girls probably know how that is." Why was she telling us all this? It was like she was trying to sell us on the idea of being her kids. How had it ever gotten that far?

"Mr. Reeve and I have worked very hard to build a comfortable home for a family. For our family, we hope. In addition to running the farm, he's a full-time welder. So he's a very busy man; when he isn't sleeping, he's working. That's almost literally true." This was beginning to sound pretty good. I was puzzled by her speech, though; she didn't talk like most of the people I knew. Listening to her was almost like reading a book or watching TV. "I run the house and tend the vegetable garden. Sometimes I take in sewing. Anyway, what I'm getting at is that we're all ready to welcome children into our home. But Mr. Reeve and I can't have children of our own."

She stopped for a while. A single tear formed at the corner of her eye. She dabbed at it, almost angrily. "Stop the nonsense, Lynette," she said, as if to herself. "I've always wanted a little Indian girl of my own. You may not think so, but I'm half Delaware. My mother was a full-blood, a Whiteturkey, and I want a beautiful Indian daughter of my own."

My eyes must have widened. A Whiteturkey? She could be Simon's aunt or something. It didn't really matter, but it sure was interesting.

"Do you know a Simon? Simon Whiteturkey?" I had to ask. "He lives here." I liked Simon. Maybe if she didn't go for us, she'd take a boy who was related.

"Well . . . that's interesting. I'll have to check on that. But no, to answer your question, the family isn't so close anymore. I've really lost my Indian family, just like you have. That's why I want to . . . Mr. Reeve and I want to . . . well, we want to make an Indian family of our very own."

The smile that accompanied her last statement was radiant. I was starting to like this woman. I figured it was time to lay my cards on the table. "Listen, you know we're not Delawares," I said. "Apaches."

"Apaches?" She said it like she'd never heard the word before. "And what are Apaches like, young lady?"

"We're the people who, when there's something bad needs to be done, we do it," I said gravely. Jackie nodded her head in vigorous agreement. "Like when there's a cat that's been bad hurt, we're the ones who put it out of its misery. I been told that in the old days we did a lot of scalping, burned houses—all that."

She didn't look terrified; she looked amused. "I see they'll need some special attention," she said to Mrs. Joseph. And me she only asked calmly, "And you've done all these things yourself?"

"I did the cat," I muttered under my breath.

"And she gets in fights all the time," Jackie added enthusiastically.

Mrs. Reeve cupped my chin in her hand and looked deep into my eyes. "From what I've heard," her voice was almost musical as she said this, "Apaches are people who put wonderful pictures on their baskets and their clothes and their tipis. Apaches are artists."

I'd never thought about that before, but I couldn't deny it. Jackie wasn't much of an artist, but she wasn't much of a scrapper either. Maybe I was the more Apache of the two, but it would be fair to say that I was something of an artist as well as a fighter.

"Mrs. Joseph was telling me that you girls are very good little artists," she went on before I could say anything. "I'm hoping that you'll both draw me a little something." She produced a blue crayon and a couple of sheets of drawing paper. Jackie proceeded to snatch the crayon and prove Mrs. Joseph at least half a liar in short order. She drew something that I recognized as Mrs. Reeve holding Jackie on her lap while the little darling sucked a big lollipop. I don't imagine either of the older women recognized much of anything in the blue scribble on the page. Plump little Jackie had stick arms and legs every bit as long as the stick arms and legs of the woman who held her. The lollipop was fully as big as the two heads. It looked most of all like a spiky desert plant with three round flowers. Mrs. Reeve held it up, gave it a careful look, and said, "Very nice, honey." I was really getting to like her.

I wanted to make her something nice, something to remember us by, in case, as I suspected, this would prove to be the last time Jackie and I ever saw her. I would have drawn a horse, but horses aren't blue, and I only had a blue crayon. The only thing I could think of that was blue was a bird. I didn't really know what a bluebird looked like, so I made it resemble the most magnificent bird I'd ever seen, an old guinea at that awful farm we'd stayed at. It was one mean bird, but it sure was good-looking. I really took pains with that bird, and when I was done, it truly was a beauty. The tail feathers were fully three times as long as the bird's body; the neck and bill looked something like a swan's.

"Why, this is beautiful, honey," she said as if she meant it. "Just what sort of bird is it?"

Well, she didn't have much of an imagination, did she? "Why it's a bluebird," I answered. What could be more obvious?

"I'll take it home. Mr. Reeve and I will cherish it." She gave me a look, as if something else had come to mind.

Mrs. Reeve left shortly thereafter, shaking both our hands, praising our good looks and better manners and promising to come back and pay us a visit soon. I hardly credited that last promise as very likely.

The very next day, the State of Oklahoma moved a big diesel shovel and a whole fleet of dump trucks onto the Bacone College grounds. They took away the burdensome job of digging foundations for our three new cottages from Phyllis and me. It looked like maybe, just maybe, both of our living arrangements could be changing pretty soon.

PHOTO
21

A LECTURE OVERHEARD

If we'd been given seats inside the lecture hall, we'd probably have nodded off. Richard West's talk is that far over our heads, intellectually speaking. But now, because his voice is literally over our heads, filtering through the open window in the brick wall that hides us, the adventure's almost unbearably exciting. A cool breeze ripples the drying leaves of the maples that are beginning to turn color, giving a whispered harmony to his deep voice, but the tremors that shake my body have nothing to do with the wind.

"My daddy painted that."

The astonishing claim, made in a voice that could have belonged to a boy or girl, took me completely by surprise.

Ever since I'd met Richard West at school and had my brief, one-sided talk with him, I'd felt a new fondness for the wonderful altarpiece at our Bacone church. After all, I knew the painter. I took to kind of holding back as we all left the church so that I could spend a few minutes studying the mural after the crowd thinned out. Some of the other orphans noticed me doing it and followed my lead. Jackie didn't have much patience for art; sometimes she hung back with me, but more often she bolted out of church to romp and race with the other young ones. Phyllis and Eunice did admire the painting; in short order they became as expert about its virtues as I.

We were looking at the epic mural as usual, discovering something none of us had noticed in the expression of one of the disciples, probably Peter, when the voice behind us made its startling claim. Now, having had the opportunity to shake Richard West's hand, it shouldn't have surprised me that he was a flesh-and-blood man who might very well have a family with kids my age, as so many men his age did. But I didn't think about him that way. So the first words out of my mouth in response to the incredible boast were, "Yeah, in a pig's eye he did."

"No, really," the boy insisted. "Arnie West." And he offered me his hand. He looked to be a little older than me, and he was dressed in a rather distinguished blue suit. A younger boy, in brown slacks and sweater, also stuck out his hand. "Ben West," he said. "It's true. We watched him."

"Now, that's a whopper." Phyllis beat me to it.

"No really," Ben insisted. "We watched. Til we got bored." I couldn't imagine ever getting bored watching a great man work magic with his brush, but then, Richard West wasn't my dad.

It turned out that the West brothers were lonely and, yes, bored at Bacone. Apparently, most of the staff who lived on campus didn't have kids. "Why don't you come and play some ball with us?" Ben invited. It was hard to resist an invitation to play ball from the sons of my favorite painter in the world. So we went along to the Wests' home and waited outside while they changed out of their suits. The boys did have some nifty play equipment: a horseshoe set, some beach balls, a softball, a couple of bats, a tire swing. That first day, we played kickball with a ball you could actually boot past second base.

We saw the brothers at church nearly every week after that, but somehow the opportunity to play seldom came up. It seemed they were busy nearly every Sunday afternoon; in any case, they went their way, and we went ours. I remember only one other time that we got the chance to play with Richard West's sons. Ben West seemed to be trying to signal us at church. When the sermon was over, Phyllis and I hung back by the altar painting. The brothers stopped just long enough to drop an invitation: "Meet us by our swing. There's something we got to tell you."

One of the nice things about meeting by the tire was that we got to swing. We had some swings at Murrow, and swinging was one of my favorite things. I climbed into the tire, wrapped my arms around the thick rubber and held on just as hard as I could, soaring up into the branches as the West boys pushed with all their might. I didn't want it to end, though I was eager to know what the important something was that they just had to tell us.

"Dad doesn't just paint, you know," Ben confided. "Sometimes he gives talks. To students, folks from the town, white people, you know. Usually Arnie and me don't go. We hear him rehearsing actually. This time we overhear your names come up." I looked at him, and he shrugged. "I don't know. We weren't paying all that much attention. Then we heard Phyllis and Linda. He's giving the talk day after tomorrow. Four-thirty in the afternoon."

"Well, where?"

"The lecture hall. Don't you know it?" A shake of the head answered that question. "Second building past the church. On the right. The brick building with hardly any windows, except that one, real high."

Phyllis and I had to do some quick chores and hard running that day, but we'd made up our minds to hear the great artist's lecture. We knelt under the lone high window. The sound of Richard West's deep, resonant voice fell on our heads like rain. What I remember hearing hardly represents his lecture. And yet, some of the words, some of the ideas, have stayed with me for years.

"We paper over the reality of things with the word *culture*. . . . What culture really means for my tribe, which is Cheyenne, and all the rest . . . our own houses, ways of hunting and fighting, religions, songs and dances, foods that we grew and gathered and cooked, clothes that we made and decorated in our own special ways. Very specifically, we all had grandmas who knew just about everything and had no end of wonderful stories. Bear with me . . . the importance of grandmas will soon come clear.

"White people came. They couldn't understand . . . so placed no value on our ways of life. Wanted us to be like them, so they broke everything that was ours. Worse, they took our children and taught them to hate their birthright. Cut off their fine hair and made them wear clothes like the ones we all wear now. And taught them from books that white is right and red is dead. I was one of those little Indian children who got a good American education. So what I have to find now is what I lost along with my long black hair when they brought me to boarding school. I'm trying to find what it really means to be a Cheyenne . . . an American Indian.

"People tell me that my work is very good because it's like the paintings white artists produce. I'm a trained ape, you see. . . . I don't want to paint like a white man with red skin. I want to paint like a Cheyenne, like an Indian.

"I want to find out what a Cheyenne should be painting if there had never been Columbus and all that followed. Maybe what I mean is that I want to find out what a Cheyenne should be painting even though there has been Columbus and all that followed. . . . When you get down to it, what all of us at Bacone are looking for now is an Indian way of painting.

"I want to tell you about two little girls who've showed me that maybe we never really lost what I supposed we'd lost. We all have grandmothers, after all.

"These girls really only have one between them. Phyllis, the little Kiowa girl, has sat at her grandma's knee. Which is a place I recommend all of us sit before we decide what Indian art is all about.

"Anyway, grandma told her the story of the Kiowa tree, with its roots in our world and its branches in the next, spanning a bottomless chasm. Well, if you don't know it, the story itself isn't the point. What's important is that Phyllis told her story to a little Apache girl. And because Linda didn't know her own Apache stories, the beautiful stories of her tribe, she painted Phyllis's Kiowa tree. But the thing that got to me is that she didn't paint exactly what she heard. She made it her own. She put horses in the Kiowa heaven, I guess because she really likes horses. She put a man in a black tuxedo playing a piano in that same heaven. For the same reason: she really likes Liberace.

"Yes, it is funny . . . in a way. But quite wonderful in another way. I'm not telling you that the tribes were childish, not at all. But they didn't have museums either. They had grandmas. They had what was alive to them, not layers and layers of dead artifacts and dead ideas choking out the living heart of their world.

"We have to get out of the museums and listen to the grandmas. If you don't have one of your own, talk to Phyllis's grandma; she has lots of stories. But the thing I've learned, I think, is that we can't worship the stories. We have to live in them and paint the life of them. We have to tell them in paint as our very own stories, those of us, whether little girls or old men, who hope to be—truly to be—Indian painters."

I'd been having a hard time following all that he said, but I heard his concluding line. I think it's about the nicest compliment I've ever been paid.

The West brothers were nice guys. I never heard their father speak again. Yet my play with the boys has faded into the mists of memory, while Richard West's lecture, the meaning of his words, becomes clearer with time. I followed his career as best I could and saw it eclipsed by others who picked up his brush, so to speak, and took it further than he could. But always the quest has been the one he defined in that lecture: to discover what it means to be an Indian artist in this oh-so-complicated world.

PHOTO

22

THEY DON'T EVEN LEAVE US OUR HAIR

Long, lustrous black hair reflects in black eyes. Dark eyes shine with a cold light when coils of thick, gleaming hair bounce and sway before them. Phyllis's cousin Helen came to Murrow with the thickest, blackest hair I've ever seen. White women of a certain age would be proud to wear her hair as a collar on their sensible cloth coats. Her hair hangs below her waist; when she combs it in front of her, it hides her face more completely than any veil; when she wears it in braids, she might be the native Rapunzel. Helen would be a pretty girl bald, but her hair is her glory.

There were adoptions at Murrow; there were also new arrivals. It was as if the old brick building breathed in and out. It was no different from other institutions, I suppose—the army in wartime, prisons at all times, corporations too, to be prosaic. The rhythm of comings and goings is a pulse of modern life; we danced our Murrow two-step to its erratic beat. So the arrival of Helen Bluecloud, a younger cousin of Phyllis Goodbear, was nothing out of the ordinary. The only thing noteworthy about it was that Helen Bluecloud was an unusually beautiful little girl, and her hair was her finest feature.

There was a cruel irony in that last fact. Beautiful smiles, finely chiseled cheekbones, full lips, slim, perfect noses, flashing eyes, sun-kissed complexions, even long curved lashes—all those components of beauty were as secure at Murrow as they were in any place subject to the ravages of time. Hair was different; hair was certain to succumb to hazards peculiar to Murrow and much swifter than time.

Life at Murrow satisfied only one of the ideals of the French Revolution. Of liberty there was precious little. Between the demands of school and chores and the military memories of Alice B. Joseph, we had to fight for every ungoverned moment. Of fraternity there was less. Murrow was an almost perfect model of Darwin's law of survival: the old preyed on the young, the strong on the weak, and the only sisterhood was among victims and outcasts. But equality we had in abundance. Ours was a society of shared clothes and shared treats from home. We called nothing our own. We wore no makeup, and our haircuts were all the same. We had few mirrors; sometimes when we looked in one, we weren't quite sure who was looking back.

Many of our girls came from rural towns in Oklahoma with the talk of the tribe on their lips and the look of the tribe in their camp dresses, their jewelry, and above all their long, black ropes of hair. They arrived scared and skittish, given to terrors and tears. Even though Jackie and I had not come from Indian country, we could remember the fearful unfamiliarity of the place, the self-effacement of the clothes line, the continual threat of the bullies, the thefts of food at table, the air of superiority worn by the girls who already knew the ropes, the tests of courage and character we were put to. In short, we remembered the initiation rites at Murrow. And central to those rites was the compulsory haircut, when the long Indian hair fell in ropes to the floor, limp, like snakes with broken necks.

The haircut was defended on grounds of practicality. Head lice were a dreaded plague, and long hair was likely to get lousy. The seeds and burrs that grew in abundance in Big Planet and the horse pasture blew into long hair and tangled. Even spiders might find their way into long hair. I don't remember anyone suggesting that bats or birds or mice might nest in a wild Indian head, but virtually all pests smaller than those were proposed in all seriousness as scourges of long hair. And yet, as Phyllis pointed out, long hair was worn by Indian girls—and boys—who lived in precisely the same rural circumstances as we did.

I bought into the necessity of the haircut wholeheartedly. With my own hair cut short, I saw no reason why any other girl should enjoy the distinctive privilege of long hair. In our time no one had ever come to Murrow with hair to compare with Helen's. I can't say exactly what was different about it, but I will tell you that some of the smaller girls loved to run their fingers through it and found any excuse to do so. I must confess that I was looking forward to Helen's haircut with eager anticipation. My skin was breaking out at the time, and it hardly seemed fair to me that I should have ugly skin and stubby hair while Helen enjoyed clear skin and the most sublime hair.

I was most surprised when Phyllis pulled me aside one evening, with a worried look on her face, to talk about Helen's imminent hair cut. "I suppose you know that old Joseph is planning to cut Helen's hair," she began.

"Well, I suppose so," I answered promptly.

"I think it's just dreadful, don't you?" she asked, knowing full well that I didn't think anything of the kind.

"I don't know," I answered. "I mean, we all have. What's so special about Helen?"

"Helen's hair is wonderful," Enid, who'd followed her cousin, put in.

"Well, what's that got to do with it?" I asked, somewhat annoyed. "The haircuts are not a beauty question. You know they're strictly a health question." Mrs. Joseph couldn't have spouted the company line any better than that.

"Well, it should make a difference," Phyllis insisted. "Beauty is not a small matter. Why should Helen give up her best feature just to satisfy some idiotic rule? We don't ask you to cut off your tiny nose."

"Hair grows back," I insisted, startled at the comparison. "I don't like it that Helen should get privileges." While I talked, I was busy wondering whether my nose really was as special as all that. I never thought of myself as having pretty features.

"Well, you know why they do it," Phyllis said with a bitterness I'd never heard in her voice.

"Sure I do," I answered. And I began to run through the list of hazards that were commonly attributed to long hair. Phyllis cut me short.

"It has nothing to do with any of that," she declared. "Richard West told us the real reason. Think about it."

I tried to, but I couldn't think of anything he'd said about hair. I shrugged my shoulders.

"They're trying to cut the Indian out of us. That's what he said, and it's true. They don't want us to be Indians; they don't value it."

I had to interrupt. "Whattaya mean? They're Indians here. Mrs. Joseph is Indian." It was true, after all.

"That's just what Mr. West was trying to tell us," Phyllis snapped back, triumphant. She'd done some thinking about this. "Mrs. Joseph came to a place like this. A school probably. They cut her hair just like they cut his, like they cut all our hair. And she bought it all, the reasons they've been trumping up since forever to justify what they do to us. So she stopped being Indian. She hates Indian as much as any white lady could."

I didn't think that was fair to Mrs. Joseph, and I was really surprised to hear it coming from Phyllis, who was always known around Murrow as Jo's girl. There were two possible reasons: Richard West's talk had gotten to her, or she just didn't want Helen to have her hair cut. Probably a little of both, but she knew the rebel in me would more likely be moved by a cry for justice than by a pretty girl's vanity.

I was torn. I mean, I didn't actually want long hair for myself; I'd never worn it that way, and I didn't think it had much to do with my being Apache. The cat sure hadn't thought so, anyway. And I really didn't have a lot of sympathy for Helen. She seemed like a nice enough girl, if a little weak, and I thought she was being pretty much of a wimp about the whole hair issue. Come on, we'd all gone through a lot worse than that. I guess I wanted to see her hair lying in loose coils on our cutting-room floor.

"I don't know what you want me to do about this," I protested. "I mean, it's gonna happen. You should just get your cousin ready for that."

It turned out that Helen was ready for *something*: to play a big scene for me. She came rushing into the room, and I mean she was crying real tears. She started begging me to help. "My Kiowa name means Hair Like Black Rain. If

119

they cut my hair, it's like they cut my name off. Oh, please, won't you talk to Mrs. Joseph? I don't see why I can't be an Indian in an Indian orphanage." She looked at me like somehow or other all this was my fault.

"I don't know why you're telling me all this," I had to answer. "My opinion doesn't mean a thing around here anyway."

"You are the girl who—the cat girl. That's right, isn't it?" she insisted.

I just shrugged my shoulders and turned around. The question was so far out of left field that I didn't see any other way to answer it. But as I turned, I heard echoes in the room. "Yeah, Linda, you're the one. You've got nerve. Maybe she'll listen to you."

I knew Mrs. Joseph wouldn't listen to me for a minute, but that wasn't really the point. This was the first time I came to realize just how dramatically my status had changed at Murrow since that moment under a blazing sun when I had brought the rock down on the head of a mangled and dying tabby cat.

Phyllis and Linda—it wasn't a secret friendship anymore. It was a very public pairing of what had always been the most and least popular girls at Murrow, now on equal footing. We'd been mentioned in the same breath by Richard West. And now we were expected to walk together into Mrs. Joseph's office in order to reverse a policy of long standing.

That's exactly what we did. Phyllis did most of the talking, and it wasn't much. Mostly I just nodded in assent. Mrs. Joseph listened in astonishment; she'd probably never been formally challenged on a matter of policy in all her years of running things at Murrow. Phyllis was by no means as forceful and eloquent with the old lady as she had been with me. "Her hair is just so beautiful" and "I can't see what's so bad about looking like an Indian" were the only strong statements I remember her making. Mrs. Joseph did us the courtesy of explaining the policy yet again. She told us that Helen was just too young, that only the big girls got to wear their hair long. And she finished by saying, "It would be more unkind to the girls with short hair to let Helen keep hers." As if Indian girls, unlike all others, had to look alike. As if we all had to look plain. Even though I felt myself to be plain, I didn't much like that.

A couple of days after our protest, Helen's lovely long hair went cascading to the floor in heaps. She brooded about it for a couple of days, then went on to other things. I always suspected that the main reason Phyllis wasn't one of the very first children invited into the family cottages was because she did what she did and said what she said in defense of Helen's beautiful hair.

PHOTO

23

ICE CREAM OUT OF SEASON

It is more like a general store than an ice-cream parlor. There are screws and nails and hammers and such on one wall. Barrels full of pecans, potatoes, onions, squash, and other produce from outlying farms stand prominently on the floor. There also is a sign in the window that says "Ice Cream" and a refrigerator with big round canisters containing chocolate, vanilla, and strawberry. We stand in front of the ice-cream counter—Jackie, Mrs. Reeve, and me—lined up like a triple-decker cone. "The girls would like some ice cream," Mrs. Reeve says in her soft, firm voice. When no one answers, she goes on, "They want one dip of chocolate; I'll take strawberry—all on sugar cones." I don't have much hope for a good outcome; I've been taken to this ice-cream place before. The big, square-shouldered man behind the counter makes no move to comply with our request. Mrs. Reeve repeats the order exactly, in a tightly controlled voice. "Sorry lady," the big man says at last, "we don't serve their kind." Mrs. Reeve looks like she's been punched in the gut. The color goes out of her. You can tell that she's heard stuff like that way too often in her life. She takes us by the hand and turns to leave. "Come on girls," she says, "I know where we can go to get some good ice cream."

Unlike all the others, Mrs. Lynette Reeve came back after our first meeting. The second time, she brought peanut-butter-and-jelly sandwiches made with a very good, homemade jelly, crayons, and a pad of paper. The manilla paper had those thin blue lines, which made it hard to draw on, but it was way better than what I usually had to work with, and I was happy to get it.

Mrs. Reeve brought me something else on that second visit: a new name. "I really liked that bluebird you drew for me last time," she told me. "In fact, it's taped to our refrigerator right now. I was so pleased that I asked my mother what the Indian name—I should say the Delaware name—for 'little bluebird' is. She told me the word is *okee-chee*. *Okee-chee*—that means 'little bluebird' in the language my people speak, in Delaware. If you don't mind, I would like your Indian name to be Okee-Chee, Little Bluebird."

I nodded yes right away, though I could see that there was a lot about this I'd have to think through. For one thing, giving me an Indian name seemed to mean that she expected to see more of me; there didn't seem to be any other good reason to do it. In a way, I felt like I should be consulted about such a thing, but on the whole I thought I was alright with it. Okee-Chee, Little Bluebird, seemed altogether a better Indian name than the one Helen had. Hair Like Black Rain—that was a name they could take away from you just by cutting your hair. My name was different. Once you had it, you had it.

I made her write it down for me. Okee-Chee. That didn't seem like it would be hard to remember. I wrote it again and again on a piece of paper, and by the time she went back home, I had it memorized. I think that pleased her.

The third visit launched the great ice-cream adventure, which won me over to Mrs. Reeve's side. I really admired the way she handled the whole thing. By the time we made our weary way back to the orphanage, I knew she was the woman I wanted for my mom.

The adventure started innocently enough. I guess she thought she'd been favoring me, because the first thing Mrs. Reeve did on that third visit was to pull Jackie up on her lap and say, "Okay, little darling, just what would you like to do today?"

It was already deep into autumn. Most of the leaves were off the trees, and a chill was in the air. But Jackie liked what she liked, and one of the things she liked in all seasons was ice cream. So her answer was, "Could we please go get some ice cream? I'd love a chocolate cone."

I guess Mrs. Reeve had a taste for a strawberry cone herself, or else she was determined to make this Jackie's day. The ice-cream request proved to be no easy thing to satisfy. A month earlier it would have required nothing more than a walk down the road toward Bacone. In summer and near summer the college opened up a little building at the head of the road to serve as an ice-cream parlor. The college kids could be seen strolling the grounds licking cones piled high with the most luscious triple dips—chocolate, vanilla, strawberry was the favored order. There was a standing challenge among us Murrow orphans to see who could get adult visitors to buy them the most ice cream. I think Jackie and I were about a hundred scoops behind some of the champs like Rachel, who had a lot of family visits in the summer, and Enid, who just seemed incomplete unless she had an ice-cream cone in her hand. But now we were about to come a little closer to evening the ice-cream score. Jackie and I led Mrs. Reeve down a road that seemed paved with yellow leaves, skipping along in our excitement. When we got to the parlor, we found the windows shuttered and the door locked. "Closed for the Season," a redundant sign proclaimed. Of course, we should have known. We hadn't gotten a cone in weeks; neither had anyone else.

If Mrs. Reeve had let it go at that, Jackie and I would have understood and accepted. She'd tried; the mistake was ours. So be it. But she didn't settle. She asked some of the college kids, got directions, bundled us in her car, and headed into Muskogee. She consulted notes she'd taken, circled the neighborhood a couple of times, I think, and finally pulled up in front of a little shop that looked all too familiar. We'd been there before. We'd been hurt there before. But maybe something had changed; maybe they weren't so mean there anymore. I decided not to say anything. When I saw that big, nasty man behind the counter, with his filthy apron that looked like it was saturated in layers of ice-cream stain, I knew we weren't getting any cones from that place. But I wasn't really all that interested in the ice cream anymore. This had become some sort of test of Mrs. Reeve; I really wanted to see how she would handle it. Could she protect Jackie and me, or would she just lay down?

"Sorry, lady, we don't serve their kind."

I saw her eyes glaze over for a minute, the starch go out of her spine. Like there was an open wound somewhere on her and this filthy man had touched it, and it hurt. I knew that feeling myself; every "Soreface Lakoe" did it to me. But then I always snapped out of it and fought back. That's what I wanted to see her do.

She took each of us by the hand and turned to go. Her grip was weak. When we got to the door, she gave my hand a squeeze. She ushered us through the door, and then, framed by the doorway, she suddenly became the picture of a fighting saint. "I promised myself I'd never again sink to the level of vicious fools like you," she said. "But to talk to beautiful children like this in such terms is beneath contempt. You, sir, and bigots like you, are the reason why our state is considered backward and ill-bred by most of this country. Our Indian heritage should be a point of pride. Let me tell you that we wouldn't consider purchasing ice cream from your kind."

She walked out of there with her head high. He sent some curses after, but mostly they hit the floor; his head was that low. For me, her speech was better than ice cream could possibly be, but it turned out that it wasn't an either-or situation. "Come on," she insisted. "I know a place out on the highway that serves great ice cream."

We got in her old Chevy and started out down the highway. Jackie and I didn't get to go driving very much, except on that same old school-bus route day after monotonous day. What a lot of cattle there were out on the Oklahoma prairie! I'd forgotten how exciting it could be to see a big, milling herd of Angus or longhorns, some of them wading belly-deep in the little water holes that dotted the countryside. There was a nice roll to some of the land, and the trees that lined the little streams stood tall in the sea of waving brown grass. Heaps of hay lay in lines like bloated memories of buffalo on some of the fields. I didn't know what they were and finally asked. Mrs. Reeve laughed a quick, warm little laugh as she answered, then proceeded to point out features of the countryside. "See that hill?" she pointed at a hazy, flat-topped hill on the far horizon. "That's a mound. It's not a natural hill: people made it, ancestors of the Osages, maybe, one of the local tribes." I guess I looked blank. "Our people—Indians—made it. They made a lot of the little hills that rise up from the flat fields around here, I believe, but certainly that one. Even white scientists agree on that."

It was pretty far away, and it looked like it must be really big. "You mean Indians made that hill? Honest?" I didn't see how or why people would make a hill. Especially Indians, who, so far as I knew, had never done anything very impressive.

"Yes, your people, your kind, as that wicked man said, our Indian people—we made that hill. And lots of others. That's why it makes me so darn angry when an idiot like that ice-cream man says something so ignorant. Our people were making hills while his people were living in caves and holes in hills. And why did we make such great mounds of earth? Because we wanted to build our houses and temples as close to the sky as possible. We came from a place with hills to a place that was flat, so we built up our own hills. Isn't that wonderful?"

You know, when she put it that way, it did seem wonderful. But how? I didn't understand that. "Well, did they have bulldozers and things back then?" I had learned something from watching the construction at Murrow, after all.

"No, honey. That's the truly amazing part. Then didn't have any motors like we have today. They had to carry dirt in baskets, probably on their heads. It took lots and lots of people lots and lots of years to do it. All working together. And nowadays we have so many men like that ice-cream guy, who can't work together with anyone, who do nothing but pick fights."

I thought about that. The idea of hundreds, thousands of people carrying baskets full of mud, enough to make a hill that would last hundreds of years, did seem astonishing, and in a weird way, wonderful. "Did our people . . . did Apaches make hills like this?" I had to ask it.

"Oh no, honey," Mrs. Reeve smiled, dashing my hopes. "Your people lived in the high mountains, far, far too high for people to have built. Your people lived up where the spirits of the mountains live. As close to the sky as any people have ever lived."

I'd never talked to anyone who knew so many things. Mrs. Reeve began pointing out birds that perched on the power lines running along the highway;

they were gathering in preparation for the winter migration. She knew all their names. I hadn't even realized that they were different kinds before she began to point them out. This was the most fascinating car ride I'd ever been on; I didn't want it to end, even if it were to end in the biggest, finest ice-cream cone I'd ever eaten.

And that's exactly where it did end. The car pulled into a parking lot in front of a not very promising wooden shack. Mrs. Reeve hurried us inside; we'd spent all day in search of ice cream, and the sun was beginning to set. "Pat, before you close," Mrs. Reeve almost shouted, "these girls have come a long way for some of your ice cream. Triple-dip chocolate cones, please."

Triple-dip! Jackie and I had never had triple-dip cones before. We sat at a picnic table and ate our way through layer upon layer of the richest ice cream I've ever tasted. The cold, cold chocolate seemed to penetrate the roof of my mouth. I could taste it in my ears, in my eyes. My whole head was taken over by the sensation of chocolate.

We sat in the lengthening shadows of evening and watched a flaming sun set behind a jagged horizon of low hills, some of them undoubtedly made by our own Indian people. The cold filled my throat, but it never reached my belly. My gut was warmed by the certainty that I had found my mother.

PHOTO

24

I EVEN THE SCORE

There is a silence that's thrilling. The silence of an expectant crowd. A bullfighter must hear it at the moment of truth, sword poised for the kill. A sprinter set to race, waiting for pistol shot. A basketball player at the free-throw line, game tied, no time on the clock. A pianist as the conductor stands, baton in hand, ready to call the orchestra into sound. I hear it in the Murrow yard on a cool, clear day in November. I stand facing Rachel, ringed by every boy and girl at the orphanage. Just me and Rachel, not four of her friends, or six, or a dozen. The two of us, girl on girl, in the confrontation that's been building since the day Jackie and I first came to Murrow. She has something balled up in her right fist. I close my eyes. I smell the dirt in my nose and taste it on my tongue. I dance to my left and feel her rush by me on the right. I open my eyes, which are working fine. I've weathered her dirty little opening shot, and I'm feeling fine. I know she's mine.

Maybe it began the day I walked up to a thrashing bag and did what no one else dared to do. Now, I'm not saying that Rachel and I ever got along. I think I was number one on her hate list about the day I walked into Murrow, and it didn't take her very long to rise to the top of mine. Even so, something changed about the time I put the cat out of its misery. Maybe she started to see me as something more than this skinny little nuisance. Maybe she got jealous of the new respect that was coming my way. I don't know; I haven't spent too much of my life speculating about the motives of people like Rachel.

What I do know is that just a few days after the incident with the cat, I started getting extra attentions from Rachel. She took to leaving little presents in my room—dead birds and mice, things like that. I'm not sure why; I think she knew I wasn't much afraid of them. But it is kind of disgusting to find a dead mouse under your pillow, take it from me. One time, when Jackie found a sparrow on her sheet, it took an hour or so to calm her down.

After we started seeing Mrs. Reeve, Rachel or one of her cronies would turn our room upside down following each visit on the off chance that the good woman had given us something and we were stupid enough to try to hide it in our room. That wasn't very likely.

My skin outbreaks drew a torrent of abuse and derision from her now. She pointed, she laughed, she shrieked "Soreface Lakoe" at every opportunity. Her behavior got so bad that it caught the attention of Mrs. Joseph, who went so far as to assign her a weekend's dishwashing without help. That really was a severe punishment. No one could remember anything like it, and I will confess that I got no end of satisfaction from her distress. After that she did grow more discreet, but certainly no less vicious. I knew the clock was ticking on an eventual showdown.

At about the same time, I began to plot my revenge in earnest. Now that I knew Phyllis hated Rachel and would surely be my ally, I felt confident enough to start making real plans. In fact, the best way to "get" Rachel became a favorite topic of conversation between Phyllis and me. After the fall drying and dying of grass rendered the cemetery an unsuitable meeting place, the two of us would secrete ourselves in the horse pasture to plan and scheme.

After much debate, we settled on two scenarios. The first one, Phyllis's idea, played on Rachel's pride about Osage oil. Obviously, her family had no oil money, or Rachel would enjoy better lodgings than Murrow could provide. But she seemed somehow to imagine that she shared in the wealth and accomplishment of her tribe as some sort of birthright. Because so many Osages were rich, poor, ugly Rachel was better than the rest of us. How she must long to share in the Osage birthright in actual fact! If we could convince her that there was oil out in

Big Planet, we might induce her to dig a very deep hole. How rich it would be if the whole orphanage could watch Rachel dig into the packed dirt until she was up to her eyeballs in it! But what could we tell her? How could we convince her that we'd stumbled onto an oil strike? That was a sticky question. We couldn't think of an answer. Over and over again, Phyllis and I imagined Rachel throwing shovelfuls of dirt from a hole too deep for her even to climb out of. We imagined the filthy sweat pouring off her face and soaking her clothes—thick and black, just as if it really were oil. We had some good laughs picturing Rachel being hauled up, drenched in the only "oil" on Big Planet.

Our second little drama—my idea—started with Rachel's fierce jealousy of my new notoriety. We'd goad her into beating a bag, presumably holding a cat, before a large and enthusiastic audience on the Murrow grounds. Only there wouldn't be a cat in that bag. What substitute could we find that would complete her humiliation? We ran through the liquids—red paint, ketchup, piss, bleach—that might come bursting through a brown bag to bathe her in shame. But liquids posed too many obvious problems. How could you stop them from soaking the bag, leaking out, ruining the surprise? Phyllis made a suggestion that had real possibilities: a heap of raw liver. When Rachel beat the bag with her rock—it had to be a rock, a stick might put her too far out of range—the blood would spatter all over her face and hair and clothes. We had some fun imagining all the possibilities and variations of bloodstain.

But then I got the perfect idea, one that wiped the whole liver thing right out of our minds. A big, fresh horse turd—that's what had to be in the bag. Nothing else would do. I'm a little embarrassed to remember the positive glee with which we imagined Rachel hammering on that bag of loose, ripe manure. We would have done it, too. But there were logistical problems, odor being only the most obvious. I'm sure we would have solved them in time, but there wasn't time. The conflict resolved itself, in a way at once purer and more satisfying than any of our silly plots.

It was one of those long, boring Sunday afternoons, a little too cold for the outdoor romps that got us through this dead zone in warmer days. I was sitting over in a corner, coloring with the paper and crayons I'd been able to hide, with the greatest ingenuity, against all Rachel's raids. I knew it got her goat to see me coloring, when she couldn't seem to find my treasure. And because of my new reputation, she couldn't just walk up and commandeer the prize. Her cohorts wouldn't help her; they'd acquired just a touch of respect.

Perhaps those considerations led her to make her fatal boast. "It don't take no Apache to kill a cat in a bag," she claimed, loudly enough so I'd be sure to overhear. "Where's the big deal in that? It's hittin' a bag, is all. Why, when I get done with a cat, you wouldn't be able to tell it from a big old pile of manure."

When I heard that, I couldn't keep the laughter from bursting through the rickety dam of my self-control. I tried to stop myself, but a chuckle broke through, followed shortly by waves and peals of laughter. I don't think I'd ever done anything remotely like that before. When I recovered myself, I found that I was at the center of a circle of staring, disbelieving girls. Rachel loomed over me; a couple of girls I didn't count as friends held her back. "Not here," they insisted, "not inside. It's trouble."

"Outside, Linda," she said in a voice thick with rage. "Let's settle this."

"Okay," I jumped at the chance. "Just you and me."

Rachel looked around the room. Normally, she'd never have agreed to anything like that. But she saw the same verdict written on face after face: if she wanted a piece of me today, she'd have to do it alone.

Just standing in the center of that circle, buoyed by the picture I saw mirrored in a hundred eyes and savoring the prospect of kicking snot out of my enemy, gave me a tremendous rush. Rachel bent down as if to tie her shoe. I expected some sort of cheat from her, so I was ready for the dirt she threw at my eyes. When I found I could see, and saw her big butt looming in front of me, I gave it a joyful kick. Now she had dirt on her face to match mine.

I was so much quicker that the fight was really no contest. The only trick was to keep her from getting a bear hug on me. I danced in and out, flicking jabs in her fat face until her eyes began to swell and tears squeezed through the closing slits. She put her hands up before her face in a hopeless gesture. It was my signal to go wild on her. I started flailing my arms in a relentless windmill of punches. Rachel sank to the dust, begging me to stop and wailing piteously.

I did stop. Whenever I got an opponent to the ground, it was like someone pushed an "off" button in my brain. But this was my worst enemy in the world, and I could really hurt her now. She was at my mercy, and I knew nobody at Murrow would blame me if I took my revenge. I thought about kicking her hard, like I always kick that man in my dream. But I saw her in the dust, an ugly old bully without any real friends who would never scare anyone at Murrow again. Suddenly she seemed the saddest person in the world. I felt this was the perfect moment to stop—at the depths of her debasement, before any sentiment of sympathy could kick in.

I'm not sure to this day just why I did it, but I wrapped my fingers around a lock of her coarse black hair. "Scissors," I commanded in a shrill, breathless voice. Amazingly, someone in that crowd had a pair and brought them to me. I suddenly understood that even at war Apaches were not merely bloody killers; we were artists. Indians were artists first and foremost. I cut off a lock of her hair and held it up over my head. The silence that accompanied my action was deeper and more profound than the one that had urged our battle to begin.

I walked out of that circle, alone but not alone. I felt their unspoken respect. For that moment I was queen of Murrow. Without ever hearing the word, or understanding the concept, I had counted coup on Rachel.

PHOTO
25

PRESENTS AT PARTING

I've always loved the scent of pine. Standing around the big, fresh-cut Christmas tree with all the other little orphan girls, the pine smell is brisk and heady. The twinkling strings of multicolored lights reflect on our teeth and white blouses; we look as if we're standing in a rainbow waterfall. A church lady in a green dress with a corsage of red roses and carnations pinned to her ample bosom plays Christmas carols at our piano. She's no Liberace, but she keeps time and gives us the melody. A church choir has come to pass out gifts and to entertain. They've already given each of us a box stuffed with holiday treasures—enormous red apples and oranges, nuts and delicious Christmas candy, a comb and brush, a blouse or sweater, a top, a doll, a toy horse or soldier. I haven't really checked out my box, but I wrap my arms around it and clutch it to my chest as I sing. Jackie does the same, and Phyllis, and Eunice, and even Rachel—all of us basking in the joys of Christmas. We sing carol after carol; when we get to the line "following yonder star," I tilt my head up to look at the big glittery paper star atop our tree. I'm almost dizzy with happiness.

Cold weather is very restrictive. Howling winds and blowing snows descended on the southern plains early this year, confining us to orphanage building and grounds, stripping the cemetery of cover, freezing me out of my horse pasture and Big Planet. I hated being all cooped up indoors, but a thin, threadbare coat conspired with a steady, savage wind to keep me penned in with the others. Thanks to many happy circumstances, my victory over Rachel being the latest and most compelling, Jackie and I were ever so much happier in our confinement than we had been, alien and outcast, the year before.

We enjoyed an interlude of peace under what I suppose was my protection. The bullies were at bay, and timid little girls like Enid and Eunice and Helen felt comfortable enough to play openly with their precious toys. I didn't usually join in the games of doll picnic and teatime; I occupied my space, drawing mostly and also taking on all comers at checkers, which was a favorite game of mine.

I drew endless black and white horses and many, many Christmas scenes while I awaited the holiday—trees and Santas and snowmen. I tried to repeat my drawing of the Kiowa tree, substituting a Christmas tree for the long trunk and spreading branches of my earlier effort. I wanted to give the picture to Mrs. Reeve, but I couldn't get it right. The branches and needles of the pine were too dense for anyone to walk through; that was the main problem. It just didn't make sense, and eventually I gave up on it. But I did complete some of my happiest celebrations of the Christmas season and saved them. They were the best present I could give Mrs. Reeve.

We made plans to visit the Reeve farm and meet the man who might very well become our dad. They were very involved with church and family and wouldn't be able to come and get us until the day after Christmas. That was fine with me. Last Christmas at Murrow had been the best day of my life, Jackie's too, and we didn't want to risk a known delight for any mere promise of happiness. If we could celebrate the holiday at what was, after all, our home before going to check out what might become our home, that would be the best of all possible worlds.

I'd wanted to get out of Murrow, so much so that I'd envied Ruthie her escape and even followed in her footsteps in my most desperate fantasies. But now that it looked like Jackie and I might really leave, things had gotten ever so much better at the orphanage. I had a friend; I had respect. The name Apache was no longer spoken like a curse; instead, it was a mark of honor. I had discovered a capacity for art, an appreciation of music, a heritage that was colored by beauty as well as savagery. There was more to this Apache thing—and to me—than I'd ever imagined. And some of the people who could help me in my self-discovery—Mrs. Joseph, Phyllis, Mr. Richard West—were right here at Murrow.

Then again, I'd come to believe that Mrs. Reeve knew a great deal about these matters and might be the one to lead me to myself. She'd already taken to calling me Okee-Chee—her little bluebird—and that was something I'd never even suspected was a part of my character. I liked the name, though I swore her to secrecy as to what it meant. I couldn't have anyone at Murrow knowing that I allowed myself to be called Little Bluebird.

During the darks of late fall, with the weather-enforced confinement weighing heavily on me, I started to talk about horses. For some reason that I didn't understand then, and that I understand only dimly now, the contest between black and white horses suddenly seemed terribly important to me. Mrs. Reeve had let slip the merest hint that she might have among her farm animals one lone horse. I didn't dare ask her anything about it, but I wondered and speculated without end.

"Do you think it'll be a white horse, really, Jackie?" I asked for the tenth time one day.

"If you want to know, I think it'll be a brown mule," she answered with a testiness that was well justified, though it seemed cruel to me then. "Or maybe it'll turn out to be a cow, one of those spotted cows. I don't think you'd know the difference." Now that still seems cruel to me today.

"The white horses shine in the sun," I said to Phyllis as I showed her page after page of white horses that I'd drawn. "Nothing is more beautiful in sunlight."

"The black mare in the horse pasture shines in the sunlight too," Phyllis reminded me. "And under the moon she is blacker than night."

Yes, the black was wonderful in its way, as was the white. There was no deciding between them on grounds of beauty. I filled pages with black horses too, pages of black and of white, and came no nearer a decision. How could you decide between majesties? I'm afraid I became a dreadful pest—asking and asking, debating, quarreling, never satisfied with whatever answer my poor little friends managed to give.

135

The only answer I could come up with was a wagon drawn by a team of horses, one white as milk, the other black as coal (after all, I was in Oklahoma). I drew as loving and elegant a picture of my wagon as I could and showed it to Phyllis. She looked for a minute, shook her head, and said, "Why don't you draw Santa's sleigh? It's getting to be Christmas." She was right; there was something unsatisfying about my solution. I took her advice and started drawing pictures of Santa and all those reindeer.

Before I leave the horses, I want to look back at them from a distance of years. I think that somehow the black and white horses had come to stand in my mind for two sides of my personality, of my heritage. On the one side was the girl who defeated Rachel, who put a cat out of its misery when no one else dared to do it. On the other side was the girl who loved Liberace, who drew a prizewinning picture, the girl who took a lock of Rachel's hair when I was within my rights to do much worse. I'm not saying that white horses symbolized one side of my nature to me, and black the other. There was no white and black to that. It's just that I was conscious of choices, troubled by choices, unsure that I could hold what seemed such contradictory impulses within my person. The questions about horses and the drawings of horses were the only way I could deal with these big, hard questions about my character. That's what I think about it all now.

When Mrs. Reeve came to see us the week before Christmas, I gave her quite a thick stack of Christmas drawings. She, in turn, gave me some news: Mr. Reeve would come with her to pick us up the day after Christmas. If things went well, and she fully expected that they would, he had agreed to adopt Jackie and me.

What wonderful Christmas news that was! We rejoiced always at an adoption at Murrow; we truly did. Riding far above the undercurrents of jealousy and loss was a wave of excitement and hope. Every adoption promised redemption for all the lonely little orphans. How much more, then, the adoption of the two least likely, the heathens, the Apaches!

And how poignant that promise of adoption made the week before Christmas. I didn't want to jinx things, but I had to say some goodbyes. At church on my last Sunday, I motioned to the West brothers. I hadn't really seen them since the cold weather set in, but they'd been a big part of my secret triumph, and I could never forget that. "I think Jackie and I are leaving," I said in the moment I had before their parents took them off. "We're being adopted. Really. I'll always be proud of what your dad said. Remember me." I slipped a top into Ben West's hand. I'd liberated it from the boxes of unwrapped gifts that were making their way into the orphanage. I don't suppose it was such a good thing to do in church, but it was all I had to give.

Phyllis and I had long, wonderful talks about what our futures might be. She ached to get into one of the stone cottages that were at last rising above the foundation holes we'd helped to dig. I told her I was sure she'd be one of the first ones in, that she'd get her chance to cook in a fully equipped kitchen at last. She told me how much she liked what she'd seen of Mrs. Reeve. We made the most solemn pledges to write, to call, to visit whenever we could. We swore to be friends for life and to write long, detailed diaries for each other's eyes only. We wanted always to know what the other was doing and thinking and feeling.

I'd lost too many people in my young life; I wasn't about to lose the best friend I'd ever had. We swore eternal friendship. We sliced our fingers and mixed our blood to make sure that the bond between us never broke. For all the cold weather, we revisited our favorite spots in Big Planet and the horse pasture, communed with comfortable ghosts in the cemetery, knelt beside the brick wall where we'd overheard a great man speak our names in public praise. And for all that, we felt in our bones how hard it would be for little girls to bridge chasms of distance and time. Sometimes, for all our brave talk, we'd just sit in silence and hug each other.

Christmas came like a lavish holiday cake, with a dazzling white icing of new snow. We were all aquiver with excitement, yet the day exceeded our fondest imaginings. Yellow buses full of church groups bearing gifts and wonderful food arrived at the log-cabin lodge at Bacone where we celebrated the holiday. We stood in a fidgety line while a jolly Santa handed out big boxes stuffed with gifts. Each of us went up to him, sat on his lap, and departed clutching our gift box in our arms. Mine had a doll in a lacy yellow dress, a comb-and-brush set with mirror, a jump rope, a stick puppet, a lace handkerchief, needle and thread, a play cooking set, and individually wrapped Christmas cookies and candies. Every box was different, but each was a treasure chest like mine.

After the gifting, we had a wonderful meal at the lodge. Mrs. Treat sat at the table with us; the church ladies did all the cooking today. Great, fat, browned turkeys lined up on our serving table. There were heaps of mashed potatoes and corn bread stuffing, fresh cranberries and mincemeat pies. We walked up to the long table, empty plates in hand, and returned to our places with those same plates piled high with steaming, savory food. I absolutely stuffed myself.

Food was followed by song. The church choir sang carols, then invited us up out of our chairs to sing along. Hugging our boxes to full bellies, we circled the great tree and sang as sweetly as we could. We didn't have much voice left when we finally waved the last yellow bus goodbye.

That evening, tired and contented as cats who'd lapped up bowls of cream, we sorted through our treasure boxes and exchanged gifts. I gave my cooking set to Phyllis and my comb and brush to Helen. In turn, I got a checker set and a little wooden rocking horse. Most of the other girls made similar exchanges. Somehow Phyllis had gotten hold of a little, leather-bound diary, which she wrapped with pink ribbon and handed to me with a conspiratorial look. I hadn't been able to get anything nearly so wonderful for her. So I slipped out of the room for a minute and returned with one of my precious porcelain ponies, wrapped as neatly as I could in a bit of tissue paper.

When she unwrapped the paper, I could see that she was surprised and delighted that I'd parted with another of my treasures. Now she had nearly as many of the ponies as I had myself. "I love you, Linda," she whispered in my ear. "Merry Christmas. And don't forget the diary; I have one too." I believe that when we went to bed that night, visions of sugarplums truly did dance in our heads.

PHOTO
26

A PROBLEM SOLVED, A NEW LIFE BEGUN

Jackie and I are snugly tucked away in the big back seat of the old Chevy, pillows under our heads. We've wound our way along highways, from four-lanes to two-, like salmon swimming up rivers and ever-narrowing streams toward a dimly remembered home. Now we turn off the highway right into a steep grade on cracked asphalt without benefit of a center line. Mrs. Reeve turns to us and smiles. "Up the Parker," she says, as if that explains something. The ascent squeezes us into the back seat. We make the top of the hill, go just far enough to catch our breath, then plunge down an even steeper grade. "Down the Lucy Lewis," she says with laughter in her voice. "In these parts, girls, the hills have names." The road, turning to gravel for one short stretch, plunges deeper into Oklahoma ranch country; herds of cattle press in on us from both sides. At last we slow and turn right onto a rutted gravel path. A little white house stands up on the hill that commands the pasture. I have the strongest feeling that something unexpected and exciting awaits me out in that pasture. I look just as hard as I can, but only the great iron grasshopper of an oil pump interrupts its emptiness.

I looked out our window to see a big, old, maroon Chevy pull into the lot. The two front doors opened almost at once. Mrs. Reeve stepped out on the right, and the tall, thin man who must be her husband unfolded through the door on the driver's side. They stood for a moment, holding hands and looking more than a little like Grant Wood's *American Gothic*, then walked hesitantly to our door. In just a few minutes I heard Mrs. Joseph rushing up the stairs. The good woman truly was excited for us; in fact, hers was the only face that wore a smile during the brief interview that followed.

Mr. Reeve was a man of few words and stern countenance. Mrs. Reeve introduced us, and we offered our hands, as we'd been instructed to do. Mr. Reeve extended his hand; I was surprised to feel how calloused and work-worn it was. "It's a pleasure to make the acquaintance of you young ladies," he said, though "pleasure" was not the name I'd have given to the look he wore.

That was the last word he said until we settled our bags and our bottoms into the sturdy Chevrolet and drove away from the Bacone campus. Mrs. Reeve began to babble about all the people we'd meet and the nice things we'd do on our visit. I didn't pay much attention; what I heard in her voice was a nervousness that I didn't quite understand. Once we hit the highway, Mr. Reeve seemed to loosen up a little. "I hope you girls have some good hog-slopping clothes packed up," he said. "We're gonna see just how well you young ladies can slop our hogs."

"Oh, Gordon," Mrs. Reeve said in an exasperated tone. "I don't think these girls appreciate your sense of humor."

Before she could get any further he broke in. "Got about five hundred hogs. Big, mean ones, some of 'em. You girls aren't afraid of piggies, are ya?"

I guess Jackie and I both looked afraid. Our driver peered into his rearview mirror and gave a dry little laugh. That was the last he said to us for a while, as Mrs. Reeve hurriedly gave us to know that we wouldn't slop a single hog on this trip and that we would much more likely be doing traditional girl chores, like fetching eggs from the henhouse, should we decide to live with them.

I wondered a little about the lean, hard man with the strange sense of humor who might become my dad. He was strong, I had no doubt about that, and he very likely took grief from no man. Those were good things in a dad; you wanted someone who would protect you. On the other hand, it seemed like we might need some protecting from him and his deadpan jokes. But Mrs. Reeve was showing us that she could do that, and I had every confidence in her nerve and spunk. So, all in all, I figured that he would do. Judging from his hands, he did a lot of work; we probably wouldn't be seeing all that much of him anyway.

There was a little discussion up front, and the car turned off the main road. I hadn't realized that we'd been following the road to that wonderful ice-cream parlor until we pulled up to it. We didn't get triple-dip cones, only singles. And Mr. Reeve did shake his head and mutter something about ice cream at Christmastime being certifiable. But the chocolate was still wonderful. I was pleased to see that he ordered chocolate for himself; in my experience, you could usually trust someone who liked chocolate ice cream.

The more the roads narrowed, the more Mrs. Reeve seemed to know about the human history of the places we passed. It was like she was so proud of her country that she couldn't help telling you how all the place names came to be. I mean, she knew just how and when Hogshooter Creek had received its name. I felt the same about Big Planet, but that was just a little place. It seemed that the whole countryside was her Big Planet. She started telling us about some of the criminals and bad people who'd lived in this lovely, rolling farm country, and I soon got the feeling that life here might not be as boring as looked likely. But that proved to be a misconception: I can think of only one murder that occurred in all the time we lived on the Reeve farm, and that added very little excitement to our lives.

Our climb up the Parker startled me, and our plunge down the Lucy Lewis got me in the pit of my stomach. Jackie was really scared. She hugged me and the look in her eyes said, "Sis, maybe this adoption thing isn't such a good idea after all." Mrs. Reeve just laughed and said, "You girls'll get used to that soon enough."

As we rattled our way up the bumpy gravel drive, I got the strangest feeling about the empty pasture to our right. I knew that it was alive with all sorts of things. I'd soon find that it sustained over fifty head of cattle, a sizable herd of deer, plus rabbits, possums, skunks, coyotes, and an endless supply of box turtles about as big as your palm, which caused no end of amusement as they waddled their way to the scrap heap Mrs. Reeve kept for the benefit of all God's creatures. But it wasn't the hum of abundant life that intrigued me; it was one particular, thrilling creature that I somehow felt calling out to me as we drove up the road toward the trim little farmhouse that occupied the highest ground on the spread.

We brought in our things and settled down. Mrs. Reeve had prepared us a big dinner—sliced ham, bread and chestnut stuffing, whipped potatoes, cooked carrots, a lettuce salad, and chocolate fudge brownies. It was every bit as good as the Christmas meal we'd had the night before. "I bet you girls are just as full as ticks," she observed as we curled up on the couch.

The house was compact, and our room wasn't very big. But she called it our room, and that really was the important thing. The bathroom was an outdoor privy, which was a drawback; but before Murrow that was the kind of toilet we'd been used to, so it wouldn't be a hardship.

After we got all settled in and rested up from the drive, Mrs. Reeve put our coats back on us and took us to the pasture fence. "There's something I want you girls to see," she explained, "especially you, Linda."

The sun was lowering in the sky, touching the clouds with gold and drawing the cattle toward the barn and the feed troughs. Mr. Reeve stood by a gate, ushering them in with shouts and, sometimes, a slap on the rump. The cows were big when viewed up close, much bigger than I expected. But they obeyed Mr. Reeve's sharp commands without rebellion or hesitation. Even the power-fully muscled Black Angus, which I soon learned was the bull, came when called and trotted into the fenced pasture with the rest.

I looked over the herd with pleasure. They were surprisingly agile and alert, and I liked the way Mr. Reeve compelled their obedience with his voice and manner. In the distance I saw what I imagined was a tall black-and-white cow, only it didn't really look like a cow. When he'd penned and hayed the rest of the stock, Mr. Reeve joined us at the fence. "Cattle need tending in the winter," he told us. "Rest of the year they take care of themselves. Reckon you two'll need tending all year 'round." He put his fingers to his lips and let loose with a shrill whistle. The black-and-white "cow" came racing toward us. How beautifully she moved! I saw at once that it wasn't a cow at all but a pinto pony, her patches of black and white marbled in a pattern that glistened in the setting sun.

A black-and-white pinto pony—the perfect answer to my horse question. Why hadn't I ever imagined a mount that was black and white at the same time? I don't know. I guess somehow I thought the colors were incompatible. But as soon as I spotted this spirited mare, I saw that, in truth, black and white went together in a glorious harmony.

She galloped right to us. "Her name is Cindy," Mrs. Reeve told me. Jackie shied away, but I held my hand out over the fence, and Cindy came up to nuzzle me. Her muzzle felt like satin. "She's yours," Mrs. Reeve continued in a voice that seemed to echo from the nearby hills and trees. "She's yours . . . yours . . . yours . . . yours."

I staggered back at the enormity of the news but quickly ran over to my prize. I hugged her about the neck and buried my nose in hers. Cindy was mine. Now I knew I was home.

AFTERWORD

"Well, what happened next?"

Since I began to show people this memoir, I've heard that question more than a few times. I guess the short answer is, "My life happened—and that's a work in progress."

Somehow, I think the questioners are looking for a little more detail than that. To comply, I'd like to take you on a very quick tour of the years of my growing up, on the Reeve farm, near Chelsea, Oklahoma.

Yes, the adoption did go through. Until we were old enough to spread our wings, Jackie and I grew in the cozy, whitewashed, wood frame farmhouse on the hill that overlooked the hundred-acre Reeve spread. In time our folks added an indoor toilet, which never worked perfectly but certainly made life easier on cold winter mornings. We had a barn with a big hayloft out back, a chicken coop, a smokehouse, machine sheds. And, of course, we had a tornado cellar, equipped with lanterns and chairs and an abundance of menacing spiders, which we hurried to gratefully on many threatening occasions. Dad owned a big, red tractor that was his pride. In short, we were a farm family, sharing the satisfying, challenging, hardscrabble life of many small farmers in eastern Oklahoma.

The beautiful pinto pony who greeted me on my first visit to the farm—my beloved Cindy—became my exclusive mount. I groomed her and watered her and threw the heavy Western saddle on her back. After mother waved us off, urging caution, Cindy would eagerly break into a gallop when we were just out of sight, jumping the gullies and hedges on our place with the agility of a much younger horse. Riding horseback is one of the few things in my life that lived up to expectations. Sitting on Cindy's back as we soared over a bramble hedge, knowing what might happen if she faltered, was intensely exciting. It beat all the movie rides and imagined jumps at Murrow flat.

Cindy really was a pretty old girl when I first met her, and I'm pleased to think that my enthusiasm for riding kept her young. I became a really good rider and nursed the hope that Cindy and I might barrel race at the local rodeos, but I was not encouraged in that ambition. After several joyous years together, Cindy aged beyond the reach of my energy. She died, and I went on to high school and other things. She lives on in many of my paintings.

Just a word about other pets: An abundance of animals on our farm compensated somewhat for the distance from human playmates. We raised a new batch of baby chicks each season, became attached to the cute little balls of fluff, then watched them grow older and sharper of bill. I remember a majestic old goose named Holly, who'd fly at us, wings spread, mouth gaped, as we trudged up the road from school but also caressed our hair and cheeks with the soft strokes of her bill. Then there was fierce, fine Beauregard, the king of our chicken yard, who'd peck at our legs out of sheer meanness but never failed to wake us with his crowing.

The one pet who received real affection from all was the medium-sized, short-haired, all-American mutt I continue to think of as Buster the Wonder Dog. Buster defended Jackie and me and mom and the farm from trespassers, coyotes, and especially snakes. There are cottonmouths in our part of Oklahoma, and rattlers, and the news of people sickening and even dying of snakebite was commonplace. Buster was quicker than any snake; many were the times he plunged in ahead of us as we walked in tall grass and emerged with the limp body of a rattler in his mouth.

Buster's obedience and skill were valued by my dad. I'm afraid Jackie and I fell short of his mark on both counts. We maintained a respectful truce, but I believe he thought his Apache daughters remained wild at heart. Mother may have harbored the same suspicion. I suppose, looking back, that Jackie had acquired a skill at guile and manipulation, and I a defiant independence, that may have made us difficult children. Especially for a pillar of church and community like Lynette Reeve. Mom kept us on a tighter rein than I ever held on Cindy; I know now that we benefited from her guidance and protection, but back then I wasn't so sure.

Our lives, in those years, centered on three things: chores, church, and school. Although Jackie and I had worked plenty of farms in our years as wards of the State of Oklahoma, there was still a lot to learn about the demanding chores required to make our little farm run smoothly. We were older now, and we were expected to do more grown-up work. There is a technique to taking eggs out of the chicken roosts without having your fingers pecked black and blue. To cleaning out the henhouse without emerging covered in chicken bleep. To climbing up into the barn loft and pitching a bale of hay without following it down. To unbinding the hay bale without being trampled by the hungry cattle that stampede for food, smoke pouring from their nostrils in the crisp winter air. Jackie and I mastered those techniques and many more, becoming passable farmhands after a fashion.

In farm country, chores follow the seasons. One of our happiest jobs was picking pecans from the groves that abound in our part of the state. The pickers got to keep half their harvest. Our reward was more than an abundance of sweet nutmeats; we sold much of the crop and earned money to buy school clothes.

Life was more than work. On some hot summer days, mom might take Jackie and me to luxuriate down at beautiful Bullet Ford, a bend of the Verdigris River where the swift current slowed and shallows allowed swimming. Bullet Ford had offered sweet repose long before white settlers ever discovered its refreshing waters. Exploring the wild riverbank, we'd often find arrowheads and pottery shards. Indeed, these vestiges of Oklahoma's Indian past prodded us to remember our own native heritage at a time and place in our lives that was really devoted to learning the ropes of the dominant culture.

The demands of life in rural Oklahoma were presented to Jackie and me most forcibly at church. We attended the Winganon Baptist Church religiously every Wednesday and Sunday. Mother taught Bible school there and took our lessons very seriously, preparing us for the prodigious feats of memory expected of young congregants. After Bible class, she might grill us about exactly how our teacher had presented the lesson of the week. I think she wanted to prove to the predominantly white congregation that her little Apache girls could be every bit as sober and serious about Scripture as any of the fair-haired, fair-skinned daughters of the church.

The Winganon Baptist Church was much more than sermons and Scripture for us. It was picnics and potluck dinners and box socials, baseball and horseshoe games, buses to the rodeo, regular visits to the homes of the sick and infirm, joyful celebrations of births and weddings, great somber feasts at funerals. The church was the heart and soul of our community—our mental-health service and welfare agency, the source of support for the virtuous and condemnation of the wicked. For us, it was the center that held.

Our classes at school were never as grimly earnest as our Bible study. Jackie and I completed grammar school in a two-room limestone building that was the very model of a country school. The little kids sat at their desks in one room; grades five through eight occupied the other. A very busy husband-and-wife team presided over the school, teaching all nine classes. My mother became the cook at Waller School, presiding over a kitchen-annex and serving all of us our hot lunches. There were advantages to having mom in the school kitchen: I think maybe Jackie and I got our favorite foods a little more often than some of the other kids.

The best you could say about my grammar-school performance is that I got through it, distinguishing myself on the basketball court more than in the classroom. There were a few other Indians at Waller, but we didn't really hang out together. The unspoken agreement was that if we didn't make a big deal about being Indian, the whites kids wouldn't either. We all pretty much stuck to that arrangement.

High school, at the sizable regional schools, Chelsea High and Alluwe High, broke our innocent country camaraderie and reintroduced us to discriminations large and small. I remember particularly a pretty important contest selling school yearbooks, which I actually won. There was a lot of prestige involved with winning, a princess title too. But I was persuaded to relinquish my victory to a fairer competitor. Apparently I wasn't princess material.

I was, however, recognized in school as an artist and a highly accomplished young draftswoman. I designed my own dream houses and thought of becoming an architect. But there wasn't much money in the family for college, so that dream seemed unlikely to come true. My principal, perhaps acting out of guilt for his role in the yearbook fiasco, told my folks and me about the Institute of American Indian Arts in Santa Fe, then just a year old. Here was a chance to meet Indian students, encounter native culture, come face to face with issues of identity that had haunted me since my year at Murrow and before. And all expenses were paid. The combination was simply too good to pass up.

I bravely headed out to Santa Fe in 1964. At the institute I encountered the rich traditions of native art. I found myself at the heart of a cultural and intellectual ferment unlike anything I'd experienced before. I learned that being Indian was a prideful thing. I explored painting and theater and lived among such future luminaries of native art as Fritz Scholders and T. C. Cannon. The great Apache sculptor Allan Houser discovered that I was his cousin, took me under his wing, and reintroduced me to my Apache family.

But all that really is another story.